Praise for *Dreena's Kind Kitchen*

"Once again, Dreena Burton proves that her cookbooks should be a staple in any plant-based home. The recipes in *Dreena's Kind Kitchen* are replete with nutritious ingredients to fuel a healthy body."

—T. Colin Campbell, PhD, coauthor of *The China Study* and the *New York Times* bestseller *Whole*

"Dreena Burton's Kind Kitchen engages, embraces, and inspires every individual who steps into her extraordinary culinary world. I love everything about this book—heartfelt stories, the visual appeal, the exquisite recipes, and the compassion that is woven through every page. Whether you are just beginning your plant-based journey or are a well-seasoned plant-based advocate, this book is destined to become a cherished kitchen companion."

—Brenda Davis, RD, plant-based pioneer and author

"Your kitchen can be kind for your health, kind to animals, and kind to the planet. And now, enjoying a kind kitchen is easier (and more delicious!) then ever, thanks to Dreena Burton's brilliant gem of a book. You'll find mouth-wateringly delicious (and incredibly nutritious) recipes, and practical tips to help you implement and love your kind and healthy lifestyle. This book is a road map to a happier, healthier, and tastier future."

—Ocean Robbins, CEO of the Food Revolution Network and author of *31-Day Food Revolution*

Also by Dreena Burton

Plant-Powered Families
Let Them Eat Vegan!
Eat, Drink & Be Vegan
Vive le Vegan!
The Everyday Vegan

Dreena's Kind Kitchen

100+ WHOLE-FOODS VEGAN RECIPES TO ENJOY EVERY DAY

Dreena Burton

BenBella Books, Inc.
Dallas, TX

BenBella Books, Inc.
10440 N. Central Expressway
Suite 800
Dallas, TX 75231
www.benbellabooks.com
Send feedback to feedback@benbellabooks.com

BenBella is a federally registered trademark.

Printed in the United States of America
10 9 8 7 6 5 4 3 2 1

Library of Congress Control Number: 2020058103
ISBN 9781950665921 (print)
ISBN 9781953295439 (electronic)

Editing by Claire Schulz
Copyediting by Karen Wise
Proofreading by Lisa Story and Ashley Casteel
Indexing by WordCo Indexing Services, Inc.
Text design and composition by Aaron Edmiston
Cover design by Sarah Avinger
Cover photo by Sarah Amaral Photography
Printed by Versa Press

Special discounts for bulk sales are available.
Please contact bulkorders@benbellabooks.com.

To my mother, whose strength of spirit is surpassed only by her kindness.

Contents

Foreword

By John Robbins, best-selling author and President, Food Revolution Network

Not that long ago, plant-based eaters were found mostly on the fringe or margins of society. They were typically tolerated, but they were rarely appreciated. Most people considered plant-based diets to be just another dietary fad.

And a particularly annoying one, at that.

In 2015, a study looked at attitudes toward vegans and vegetarians compared with attitudes toward other groups of people who experience prejudice. The authors concluded that "only drug addicts were evaluated more negatively than vegetarians and vegans."

But now, look at how fast things have changed!

In recent years, interest in plant-based eating has been skyrocketing. Now you can find plant-based milks in the dairy section of almost every supermarket and grocery store, often outselling the dairy options. And now you can find plant-based burgers at almost all the major restaurants and fast-food chains.

According to a report by the research firm Global-Data, in 2014, 1 percent of US consumers were vegan. But in 2017, only three years later, that number had risen to 6 percent. A 600 percent increase in veganism in the US in only three years would have been a stunning development if it had stopped there. But it didn't. In fact, the growing interest in plant-strong eating has only continued to increase and expand since then.

It's not a fad. It's not just another food craze. Scientific inquiry has produced a compelling, convincing, and coherent wave of studies demonstrating that plant-based eating leads to greater health and vitality, and to longer lives with far less disease and disability. Whole foods plant-based eating in particular leads to dramatically reduced rates of heart disease, diabetes, dementia, obesity, high blood pressure, and a host of other problems. Meanwhile, plant-based eating happens also to be a food path that leads to fewer greenhouse gas emissions, less damage to the life support systems of the planet, cleaner air and water, dramatically reduced health care costs, and far less cruelty to animals.

There's a lot to like and a lot to love about that, which helps explain why plant-based eating has been growing so rapidly in recent years. And when the immensely popular food author Michael Pollan offered his dietary advice in seven pithy words—"Eat food. Not too much. Mostly plants"—the numbers of people eating "mostly plants," or "only plants," jumped yet another notch. As more and more people have become vegans, more and more people have also been shifting from a meat- and dairy-heavy diet to a flexitarian one.

Which brings us to this beautiful book by the plant-based cookbook author Dreena Burton. For years, she's been showing people how to prepare foods that are beautiful, lush, nutrient-rich, colorful, exciting, abundant, and above all, delicious. And this may be her finest and most useful offering ever.

Dreena began her plant-based journey gradually, taking it a step at a time. And she did so when there were no vegan cheeses, no dairy-free ice creams, and no plant-based meats.

But she kept going because her body had never felt better. And because she had a deep appreciation for the fact that her food choices were now no longer causing harm to animals or the environment.

As Dreena wrote cookbooks that were widely read and used and loved, she acquired the remarkable ability to help people find their comfort and joy on a healthy eating path. And this may surprise you, but her gifts went beyond just providing recipes that are easy to make, hugely healthful, and decidedly delicious.

In this book, *Dreena's Kind Kitchen*, you'll find marvelous recipes, of course. Dreena Burton has long been one of our most trusted sources of fabulous plant-based recipes, and in this book she gives you a wide variety of her tastiest and most popular and most healthful ones.

And you'll also find much more. You'll gain the tools to trust your own food intuition so you can look at whatever ingredients you might have on hand, and immediately see ways that you can quickly pull together a delicious and healthy dish without a recipe.

You'll learn how to take whatever leftovers you might have and confidently turn them into entirely new fabulous meals. For example, many of the recipes in this book contain "recipe renewal" ideas that will show you specific ways you can take a recipe and reinvent it for another meal.

You'll also learn about batch-cooking, which is one of the great keys to the plant-based food path, because batch-cooking is a great way both to save money and also to save a lot of time, while producing absolutely fabulous meals. Plus, you'll learn which recipes freeze well, which ones are good for potlucks or larger groups, and of course great ideas for holidays and other special occasions.

There's something quite special about the book you're holding in your hands right now, *Dreena's Kind Kitchen*. When you read it, when you make the recipes and play with them, you'll be enjoying fabulous healthy food. And you'll also be learning how to make your food path simpler, easier, and more fun, with meals that are increasingly delicious and optimally healthful.

That's a lot. But that's Dreena Burton for you. And that brings me to maybe the most important thing this book offers to you.

Dreena is not just a cookbook author, though she is that, and marvelously so. But she is also a wise, reliable, and compassionate human being. Get this book and hang out with her a little bit. You'll find yourself becoming kinder, more confident, and healthier. And your food path will become filled with more beauty and joy than you ever thought possible.

PART ONE

An Introduction to Eating Kindly

1
Introduction

What is a kind kitchen? For me, kindness embraces so many things related to cooking—more than one might think.

To be kind is to be generous and considerate. We can show kindness in cooking, sharing foods we enjoy with people we care about, and choosing ingredients that show compassion for other beings and for the planet. Kindness means doing no harm. In a kind kitchen, no animal products are used; no cows, chickens, pigs, fish, or other animals are exploited or killed so that we may feed ourselves and our families.

We also take less of a toll on the environment when we choose plant foods. We now know that the single most impactful thing we can do to reduce our environmental impact does not involve light bulbs, recycling, hybrid cars, or turning off the tap when brushing our teeth. It's what's on the end of our forks—or not. Reducing or eliminating meat and dairy is the kindest action you can take, one that makes the biggest difference for our vulnerable planet.

When we look deeper than the most obvious acts of compassion toward other animals and Mother Earth, we can then reflect on compassion to ourselves. If our journey to eating kindly is born out of ethical or environmental concerns, we must still nourish our bodies for long-term success with this diet. Then, there is a deeper level of kindness to our bodies. If we haven't before felt a loving connection to food, as was my experience, when we begin eating foods that are beautiful, lush, nutrient-rich, colorful, exciting, abundant—and above all, delicious!—our physical bodies respond in kind, and perhaps our energetic and emotional bodies as well.

Finally, for me personally, building community and a career in the vegan and plant-based world, kindness is key. My approach is to welcome you into my world of plant-based cooking with a slew of tips and substitutions and ideas and tricks! When we radiate compassion and enthusiasm about this way of eating and living, it attracts more interest, which helps inspire and encourage others. This is the way to build sustained change.

Kindness matters. Kind cooking matters.

MY JOURNEY TO KIND EATING

As I write this, I am sitting outside on a warm spring evening after dinner, with my feet in the grass. I hear the neighbor children giggling and playing games before their bedtime.

It brings me back to when our girls were that age and I was just beginning my vegan journey with them—and, when I remember them as little girls, I think back on my own journey to a kinder way of eating. Diet and food choices were always of interest to me. I can't say it came from a beautiful place initially. My interest in food began innocently as a child: I enjoyed experiencing new flavors and textures and just simply loved food. My parents had six children, all girls! We were a busy household, and it was a lot for my parents to manage. There were the usual sibling tensions and growing pains; we also had several deaths in our extended family. I was young, but I began to feel the impact of these life circumstances at an early age. At around age 7 or 8, I began to put on extra weight. Not a lot, but I was considered chubby. I later understood that the stresses in my home brought me to connect with food as a source of solace and comfort.

Those were the years when dieting was extremely popular. My parents, with my best interest in mind, chose diets for me to begin—sometimes on my own, sometimes with my mother. If you've ever tried to follow a diet for weight loss, you may know how the story usually goes: It went well for some time, then it didn't. Then we tried a new diet, and that went well—until it didn't. All the while I was still feeling insecure, unsafe, and simply awkward. Over the next couple of years I continued to put on weight. I can't say I was ever terribly heavy, but it was enough that it caused concern for my family.

And then, the unimaginable happened. When I was 11 years old, we were struck with a family tragedy. My father died in a helicopter crash, along with my three cousins. Life changed in inexplicable ways. I withdrew, my heart closed, and everything became dark. Two years later, my sweet grandfather (on my dad's side) passed away. He was a special soul to me, a safe space in an insecure time. As a child, it seemed like death was something to be expected every couple of years.

As I moved into junior high, my insecurities grew. In teenage-girl territory, it was survival of the fittest. (Literally.) I was never a sporty kid, and gym class caused me great grief and humiliation. I soon learned how to diet on my own, and I definitely did not have a good relationship with food.

It wasn't until I was out of college that I outgrew those diets. I also learned how to exercise at home. To this day I'm grateful for that; while that habit also emerged from feeling less than worthy, I now truly love exercise, and it delivered the gift and wholeness of yoga into my life.

Soon after I graduated from college, I discovered the book *Diet for a New America* by John Robbins. It was one of those times when you know you can never go back. I couldn't unlearn what I had read. Everything I had understood to be true about our "normal" diet—for example, that we need cow's milk for calcium, meat for protein and iron—was challenged. But I was also confronted with truths about meat and dairy production. There is no Old MacDonald on a farm with happy animals. No, the atrocities of factory farms turned out to be real and pervasive. I learned that our normal diet was actually quite abnormal. No diet should involve such health liabilities, animal cruelties, and environmental tolls.

I feel I was meant to see these things. My connection to food and healthy living was always of interest. I just didn't know how to get there.

And so the journey began. It didn't happen overnight, and it wasn't all or nothing at first. It took several months of exploring—first, trying meals without beef, then without chicken, then without fish. Finally, eliminating eggs and dairy.

My body never felt better.

Now, remember, this was in the early 1990s, in the early vegan days; Paul and I had just gotten married. *Vegan* was largely an unknown word—sometimes it even seemed like a dirty word—and the vegan lifestyle was extremely fringe. At the supermarket, there were no vegan cheeses, no dairy-free ice creams, no plant-based meats (unlike what we've seen developing in the last five or ten years). Maybe that was for the better, because I learned to cook with grains and beans, vegetables and greens, nuts and seeds. I learned how fantastic food could taste utilizing the freshest ingredients, and I discovered new flavors and cuisines through spices and fresh herbs. A whole new world of food opened up!

I also found it more enjoyable to prepare meals. Plant foods are abundantly beautiful in color, and there's a freedom to cooking and baking without animal products. No worries of cross-contamination, no greasy pots to scour. People often ask me when I became interested in cooking. While I had always been interested in food, I truly found joy in plant-based cooking. And that's when my own career as a cookbook author took off—I published my first book right around the time we had our first daughter.

When Paul and I had our daughters, plant-based parenting was obscure. Social media was just budding. I was reluctant to discuss our vegan lifestyle with our doctor, as I knew it would be met with resistance. Thankfully my midwives were understanding and helped me through my pregnancies, rather than admonishing my choices.

Not long after having our second child, I happened upon *The China Study* by T. Colin Campbell and Thomas Campbell. I remember reading it while our daughters were at an outdoor swim lesson. The sun was pouring down, the kids were laughing and splashing, and I was immersed in this book. And it's not a playful read! But it spoke to something deep within me. I knew for certain I was right about my decision. I recited sections of the book to my husband. I blogged recipes and excerpted quotes from the book. I felt such passion and connection that I wanted more people to understand what was at stake. *Just read it. Please.*

That book strengthened my conviction in eating plant-based. For me, the ethical decision behind a compassionate plant-based diet was obvious, but the health connections were not as clear. As corny as it sounds, Dr. Campbell was like my nutrition godfather. As my cookbook career flourished, I gained a reputation for being the "healthy vegan cookbook author."

MY COOKING EVOLUTION

My cooking has evolved greatly since I began my vegan journey, much like anything in life. We grow in our work, our activities, our passions. Over these twenty-five years, my cooking has certainly developed. My roots have always been in whole-foods cooking; with my first two books, *The Everyday Vegan* and *Vive le Vegan!*, I focused on whole-foods ingredients and recipes that were low in oil, and expanded my repertoire of grains and beans.

But then it became very trendy for vegan food to be indulgent. The richer, the better. More use of processed foods, more sugars and oils, deep-fried and refined. So while my work was known, it was seen as niche in the vegan community at that time. And, life as a mom of three was a sort of busy I never knew was possible! Still, I loved my work and found a way to keep developing recipes. I was still using some oils in my cooking. Not a lot, but many of my recipes included a small amount for sautéing or baking. My third and fourth cookbooks were well received, but my own personal cooking was beginning to expand.

I started to learn more about eating and cooking without oil. A friend, the well-known plant-based dietitian Julieanna Hever, sparked my interest in cooking oil-free. We connected online through our work and partnered in some events. She could see I had already developed many oil-free recipes and encouraged me to spread my culinary wings.

I already knew *some* things could be made oil-free. But could I bake a decent cake without oil? Or a fabulous pasta dish? Would my family and friends eat these foods?

I accepted the challenge!

What could I use instead of oil to bring texture, moisture, and flavor to cooking and baking? Applesauce could not be the answer to everything! (Spoiler alert: it's not!) I learned new ways to create sauces and dressings, muffins, and even cakes. As the saying goes, "Necessity is the mother of invention." I invented.

In 2015, my fifth book, *Plant-Powered Families*, was released. It was my first full cookbook with oil-free vegan recipes, and my first cookbook to focus on raising plant-based children. In addition to recipes, I shared tips on how to pack school lunches for vegan children (with an awareness of food allergies), how to navigate birthday parties, and how to get creative in those years of picky eating. This new book filled a need in the vegan cookery world, and readers loved it. Other plant-powered families soon found my Chocolate Sweet Potato Cake—and devoured it! (If you know that recipe, get ready for a fresh take on that cake on page 229—you may have a new favorite!)

Since then, so much has changed in the world of being vegan, and in my own world—not just with my cooking, but in my life. Our girls are almost grown. Now twenty, sixteen, and twelve, they are becoming their own people—and yes, they are all still vegan, and they love it!

I have also learned a great deal about myself since publishing *Plant-Powered Families*. I'm happier in my work than I've ever been. Not because of any particular achievement, but because of how I now see myself, and value myself. Two years ago I became a certified yoga teacher. Yoga has taught me more about myself than about any particular pose!

I love to create just for the enjoyment of the process, and what it brings to those I share it with.

I am grateful for where I am today. With my work. With this book.

I hope this book inspires you. I hope that you are excited to try my recipes in your own kind kitchen. But beyond the recipes, I hope this book gives you the tools to trust your own food intuition so you can look at ingredients you have and imagine ways to quickly pull together a dish without a recipe. Or, to spot that container of leftovers and have the confidence to combine it with other ingredients, repurposing it to create a new meal.

Finally, I hope these recipes fill your heart as much as your belly. Kindness in one area of our lives spills into another. If we connect to kindness on our plate, that connection manifests more kindness in our relationships—to our loved ones, community, planet, animals, ourselves.

IN THIS BOOK

You'll find more than recipes here. The first part of this book is designed to "prep" you for ease and efficiency in plant-based cooking.

In chapter 2, I discuss simple steps that take you from the grocery store to the chopping board, and how to use batch-cooking to your benefit. (As you'll see in my recipes, batch-cooking is a big part of bringing together daily recipes and meals.) Chapter 3 is like a kickstarter for anyone newish to plant-based cooking. You will find a comprehensive list of answers to questions I get time and time again from my readers. They ask about certain recipes, substitution, food storage, and so on.

Then, we dive into the recipe chapters! I really put my heart and soul into these recipes. I created them to be wholesome, to include vegetables in new and creative ways, and to offer flexibility for the home cook.

With each recipe you'll see notes that offer extra information about the ingredients, ideas for substitutions, and serving suggestions. Further, in many recipes I share "recipe renewal" ideas. When I'm asked how to use leftovers of any given recipe, readers are often surprised at how many ways they can take a recipe and reinvent it for another meal. In time, you'll find that this is how we can enjoy more ease in cooking. For instance, what might seem like a scrap cup of leftover soup can be reworked into a sauce for a fabulous pasta dish. In time, I expect you will create your own inspired renewals—and you'll have to share those wonderful ideas with me! With all of these notes, it's my goal to help coach you through a recipe, as if I'm doing a virtual cooking lesson with each and every one of you.

Finally, I often hear from readers "I wish there was a list of which recipes freeze well." Ditto for which recipes are good for potlucks, and of course holiday favorites (beyond what's in chapter 8, Holiday Fare), so don't miss my Recipe Picks section on page 256 for those suggestions.

With that, we begin! From my kind kitchen to yours . . . enjoy!

2
From Grocery Store to Chopping Board

Get Savvy with Ingredient Prep and Batch-Cooking

I must admit I am not always the most organized person in the kitchen. While I keep things overall in check, there are definitely areas that are in shocking disarray (hello, spice cabinet and leaning tower of food containers!). I get organized, and then it needs desperate digging-out a couple of months later. Anyone else relate? If other family members are putting things away, or if we are rushing, the organization just gets blurred. Part of life!

But there are a couple of areas that I stay in routine with: washing produce after shopping, and batch-cooking. Before you crack open a cookbook or turn on a burner, you can save time in the kitchen by advance prepping ingredients.

PREPARING YOUR INGREDIENTS

Preparation time is time very well spent. While it's not the fun and creative part of cooking, it gets you set for success with recipes. And then that time cooking is much more enjoyable.

Washing Produce

When I return from grocery shopping, I separate out produce I can wash straight up. First, if you aren't washing your produce, please start doing so. Consider how many steps that produce took before making it to your grocery bags—how many hands it has passed through, and even the contaminants on checkout belts.

This is not to make you paranoid. It's simple food safety. Produce surfaces can be extremely dirty. For instance, think about a honeydew melon. If you cut through the rind into the flesh without washing it, any surface dirt and bacteria carry into the flesh of the melon. It's not an issue of removing pesticides from nonorganic items, it's more about food cleanliness—just as you clean your kitchen surfaces and dishes. That ounce of prevention is well worth the effort.

The process is simple. Fill your sink with warm (not hot) water, with a couple of drops of natural dish soap and a splash of vinegar, if you like. Remove any stickers from the produce. Add them to the sink, give a quick wash, and then rinse and place in your dish drainer or some large strainers. You don't need to scrub the produce. Rather, gently wash and rinse. If you have a lot of produce to clean, you might want to work in batches, refilling the sink a couple of times. When washing your produce, start with the hardier/heavier items: carrots, celery, melons, or unripe avocados. Wash and rinse those first, then place in your empty dish drainer. The next produce to follow might be bananas, cucumbers, and apples. Finally, the more delicate produce items go on top, such as tomatoes, grapes, peaches, ripe pears, or ripe avocados. When I wash grapes, I use a strainer and place that right on top of all the other produce below. Similarly, if I have a dozen or so tomatoes or plums to wash, I use a strainer to hold them for drying. Let the items air-dry as long as possible. If you have a kitchen window nearby, prop it open. If the produce isn't dry when it's time to store, pat dry with a clean dish towel. Items in a strainer (such as grapes) can be refrigerated in the strainer (tap out any extra moisture before refrigerating and set the strainer in a shallow bowl). Any items being kept at room temp (see Storing Produce) can be left to dry overnight in the drainer, or patted dry and placed in produce bowls on the countertop.

So, what *do* I wash? Anything that is resilient to advance washing, including:

- apples
- avocados
- bananas (yes, bananas!)
- beets
- bell peppers
- cabbage (whole compact heads)
- carrots
- celery
- citrus fruits (lemons, oranges, limes, grapefruits)
- cucumbers
- eggplants
- grapes
- kale and collard greens: do not use dish soap, just a touch of vinegar, then spin-dry.
- mangoes
- melons
- papayas
- pears
- pineapples
- stone fruits (peaches, nectarines, plums, apricots)
- tomatoes
- winter squash
- zucchini

What you shouldn't wash in advance:

- berries: rinse before eating
- loose-leaf cabbage (such as bok choy)
- cauliflower and broccoli: rinse before eating or cooking
- cherries: rinse before eating
- green beans and snow peas: rinse before eating
- lettuces: rinse before using and spin-dry
- mushrooms: never rinse or soak, just wipe with a damp towel
- onions and green onions: rinse before using

Not only will this save time when it comes to recipe preparation, it will also expedite snack and lunch prep. Your veggies and fruit are fresh, clean, and ready to assemble for lunches and snacks at home or to pack for school and work.

Storing Produce

This list will help you store produce to get the best flavor and extend its life.

Room Temperature (countertop)

- avocados: refrigerate once ripened
- bananas
- citrus fruits (oranges, lemons, limes, mandarins, grapefruit): refrigerate if needed to extend storage
- mangoes: refrigerate once ripened
- pears: refrigerate once ripened
- pineapples: refrigerate once ripened
- stone fruits (peaches, nectarines, plums, apricots): refrigerate once ripened
- tomatoes: refrigerate once ripened

Refrigerator

Some items I store loose in produce drawers (apples, cucumbers, ripe pears) and other items (carrots and bell peppers) I store in partially open food storage bags. Try partially opened storage containers, or silicone storage bags as alternatives to plastic bags.

- apples: some people prefer to keep apples on the countertop, but I find they stay crunchier when chilled
- avocados: refrigerate once ripened
- beets
- bell peppers
- berries: rinse only when expecting to consume within a couple of days, then store in a strainer or open container with a paper towel to catch extra dampness
- broccoli
- cabbage
- carrots
- cauliflower
- celery
- cherries: rinse only when expecting to consume within a couple of days, then store in a strainer or open container with a paper towel to catch extra dampness
- citrus fruits: refrigerate if needing to extend storage
- corn
- cucumbers
- eggplant
- fresh herbs
- fresh beans (green beans, snow peas, snap peas)
- grapes: rinse only when expecting to consume within a couple of days, then store in a strainer or open container with a paper towel to catch extra dampness
- green onions
- leafy greens
- mangoes: refrigerate once ripened
- melons
- mushrooms
- pears: refrigerate once ripened
- pineapples: refrigerate once ripened
- radishes

- stone fruits (peaches, nectarines, plums, apricots): Refrigerate once ripened.
- summer squash/zucchini
- sweet potatoes: Refrigerate only in hot months, otherwise store in pantry.
- tomatoes: Refrigerate once ripened.

Pantry

These items need a cool, dark place like a garage, basement, or other pantry area.

- garlic
- ginger root
- onions
- potatoes
- winter squash
- sweet potatoes: Refrigerate in hot months.

BONUS POST-SHOP PREP: PANTRY

Many of us plan our grocery shopping with a list of food for the coming days or the whole week. When you bring those items home, what do you do? If you're like most people, you tuck everything into the fridge or pantry without much thought. But if you invest ten or twenty minutes in a few steps, it can save you time and effort when cooking crunch time is on.

Store items in an organized way that works for you and your kitchen setup. All cans of beans in one area. All tomato products on one shelf. Condiments on one shelf. Dried grains and beans in one area, nuts and seeds in another. Same for cereals and pasta. Then when it comes time to find what you need for a recipe, or to plan grocery lists, a quick glance will let you know what you have and what you need.

Chopping and Prepping Fruits and Vegetables

If there's a half a watermelon or honeydew in our fridge, no one cuts into it. But if I take five minutes to remove the rind, cut wedges, and pop them into a container . . . it's an easy grab to snack on. So, batch-prep some veg and fruit that you know your family will reach for if they see it. As we know, humans like fast food! For snacking, have grapes washed and stored in a bowl; melons and pineapples can be cut into wedges or chunks with the rinds removed. Carrots and cucumbers can be cut into snackable sticks, and cherry tomatoes can be washed and ready to eat.

In addition to snacking, it's also of course most helpful to have many produce items prewashed, cut, and ready to cook in recipes. For instance, if you know you regularly use carrots, celery, and bell peppers for soups bases and stir-fries, chop several cups by hand or using a food processor. Store in airtight containers. Broccoli and cauliflower can be chopped into florets, and kale leaves can be stripped from their stems and chopped to add to salads or soups.

Freezing Produce

As with prepping some produce items for quick snacking, you can also freeze prepped fruits and vegetables.

Overripe bananas can be peeled, sliced, and transferred to containers or bags to freeze for smoothies, pancakes, or baked goods. Other very ripe fruit can also be frozen to minimize spoilage. If berries, pineapple, or melon are past their prime, or you have a few too many ripe mangoes, just prep in chunks and freeze. Then you can use them in baking, jams, or smoothies.

Some vegetables freeze well, others not so much. Winter squash freezes very well raw or cooked. Other vegetables, like bell peppers and broccoli, take on a watery and spongy texture after being frozen. That's not to say you can't freeze them. If you aren't too fussy about that texture, give it a go. Or use them in a pureed soup or sauce, where the texture will not be noticed. Consider freezing seasonal favorites (such as corn and fresh herbs) to use later when they aren't as plentiful and are far more expensive!

Keeping Citrus Zest

I love using fresh lemons, limes, and oranges in recipes. The juices add tang (and natural sweetness in the case of oranges) and acidity, and the zest a punch of vibrant citrus flavor. I recommend organic citrus for zesting. Here's a solid tip: When organic citrus is on sale, stock up! Wash the fruits first (see page 7), then zest them and store the zest in an airtight container in the freezer. That way you can have vibrant organic zest on hand at any time. Then you can juice the fruits (it's much easier to zest first and then juice) and store that in the freezer, too, in an ice cube tray if you like. You can use nonorganic citrus for collecting extra juice, if needed.

BATCH-COOKING

Do some advance prep when you can in the way of batch-cooking. You'll notice that my recipes sometimes call for ½ cup of cooked potatoes or 1 cup of cooked brown rice. Those might seem like odd amounts to prepare for any given recipe. They are . . . if you have to prep them solely for that recipe. However, when you batch-cook ingredients like potatoes, sweet potatoes, and grains, these items are at your fingertips in the fridge (or a quick thaw from the freezer).

Because I use these precooked and prepped ingredients often in my recipes, let's cover exactly what I'm talking about.

Potatoes and Sweet Potatoes

My preferred method for cooking potatoes is a simple oven bake. You can also steam potatoes or cook them quickly in a pressure cooker. Whichever method you choose, always cook more than you intend to use for any given recipe or meal. I use small amounts of cooked red or Yukon Gold potatoes in everything from dressings to burgers, and sweet potatoes in everything from waffles to dessert! Having several sweet and white potatoes cooked and ready for use will be immensely helpful for your recipe prep. If they are still in the fridge after four or five days, use them in a big salad bowl or check the index to scan recipes where you can use them!

Since I love to oven-bake potatoes, here is my quick how-to:

For sweet potatoes (orange, yellow, purple): Preheat the oven to 425°F or 450°F. Give the potatoes a quick wash and place on a rimmed baking sheet lined with parchment paper (to catch any drips).

Don't pierce the potatoes, as they will ooze juices while baking. Bake for 40–60 minutes or even longer, until soft (baking time will depend on the size of your spuds).

For white potatoes (Yukon Gold, red, russet): Preheat the oven to 425°F. Give the potatoes a quick wash and scrub any spuds that are particularly gritty. Pierce in a couple of spots and place on a rimmed baking sheet (or as I do, directly on oven racks). Bake for 45–60 minutes, until there is no resistance when pierced with a skewer or fork.

Grains

In these recipes, I default to brown rice most often. This is for simplicity for your preparation. If you prefer to use other grains, you can experiment, but the results will differ.

Besides the recipes in this book, you can get into a routine of batch-cooking the grains you eat most often. Whether rice, millet, quinoa, or buckwheat, prepare more than you expect to eat in one or two meals. Cooked grains will keep for about five days, refrigerated in an airtight container. If you open the container frequently, they will spoil more quickly. You will know when grains begin to turn off, as there is a very noticeable odor (the same goes for beans). If you pick up on even a faint odor, discard it immediately. Remember the adage "When in doubt, throw it out." You can also freeze grains, although the texture changes with thawing. However, if you will use those grains in a stew or casserole where the texture won't be that noticeable, freezing is a great option.

See page 259 for a useful chart on cooking different varieties of grains.

Beans

In these recipes you have the option to use canned beans or beans cooked from scratch. If you're cooking from scratch, definitely get those beans prepped ahead of time. They will last 5–6 days in the fridge, and many months in the freezer. Even lentils, which cook relatively quickly, are handy to cook ahead of time and have ready in the fridge or freezer.

See page 258 for a useful chart on cooking different varieties of beans.

Soaking and Roasting Raw Nuts and Seeds

Many of my recipes require soaked raw nuts, so it's helpful to have them at the ready in your freezer for when you are in the moment and inspired to try a recipe! Rather than soaking ½ cup of almonds or cashews for a recipe, I recommend soaking larger portions (4–5 cups). Here's the how-to:

Soaking: Put raw, unsalted nuts in a bowl and cover with water. Let soak at room temperature until they plump up and become soft enough to pierce with a fork (several hours or longer depending on the texture of the nuts). Softer nuts like cashews need as little as 2–3 hours, while others like almonds need 6–8 hours. Hot water will hasten the soaking time. Nuts become softer and also larger after soaking, as they swell from absorbing some of the water. I try not to soak nuts for any longer than needed, as they can lose some integrity of flavor and consistency when their oils break down. After soaking, drain and discard the soaking water. Dry the nuts as well as possible and store in an airtight container in the fridge for a couple of days or in the freezer for a few months. When storing in the freezer, portion the amounts you expect to use, like 1 cup or ½ cup. (Although even if you freeze larger portions, it's easy to pry out a smaller amount of nuts using a butter knife.)

I also like to keep roasted nuts and seeds on hand to toss into recipes. It's easy to do:

Roasting: Preheat the oven or toaster oven to 400°F. Spread out the nuts or seeds on a rimmed baking sheet lined with parchment paper. Bake, stirring the nuts/seeds around a few times to move the ones on the edges of the pan to the center, until they turn golden brown and you can smell a "roasted" aroma. Keep a close eye on them, however, as they take only a few minutes to get golden and then can burn very quickly. Let the roasted nuts or seeds cool, then store in an airtight container in the fridge (they will keep for months).

Pasta

Pasta seems like an unusual item to batch-cook. However, I find it really convenient to reheat cooked pasta for use in lunch bowls or to bulk up a soup. When making pasta for dinner, consider cooking an extra 2–3 cups. After draining, rinse briefly in cold water (to prevent overcooking/gumminess) and drain again. Let cool, then transfer to an airtight container and store in the fridge for up to 5–6 days. If using in a soup or stew, you can add the pasta straight to the pot in the last minute or so of cooking, to soften and heat through. If using in a lunch bowl or pasta salad, you may need to rewarm/rehydrate the pasta, especially if it's brown rice pasta, which becomes rock-hard with refrigeration. To do so, put the pasta in a large bowl. Cover with boiling water, let sit for a minute or so, then drain off as much excess water as possible. Then, proceed with your saucing or seasoning!

INGREDIENT MAKEOVERS

When you start batch-cooking, you may begin to look at your staple ingredients in new ways. It's normal for us to use ingredients the same ways, week after week. Before long, food can become uninspired. It happens to us all. When you've hit a food rut, here are some ideas to inspire! And, don't miss the Recipe Renewal tips throughout this book for ways to repurpose leftover meals in exciting new ways.

Cooked Potatoes and Sweet Potatoes:

- Use wedges as "dippers" for hummus and other nutrient-rich dips, in place of or in addition to raw vegetables.
- Slice cooked potatoes thickly, season with salt and other favorite herbs and spices, then bake in the oven or toaster oven (on a baking sheet lined with parchment). Or, pan-fry in a good nonstick skillet until seared on each side.

- Top 'em! Slice larger potatoes in half, scoop out a little hollow and top with a bean mixture, leftover chili, or a little nut cheese and bake until golden and heated through. Southwest-style toppings are especially good on sweet spuds!
- Cube the potatoes and toss into a breakfast stir-fry with plenty of vegetables.

- Cut into chunks and make a rustic spud or sweet spud salad. Add beans, favorite veg, and work in a dressing. Presto!
- Give them a rustic mash and top with steamed veggies and sauce of choice.
- Slice and use as a base or topping for a casserole dish.
- Slice and add to lasagna—yes, I sometimes add sliced white spuds to lasagna! (See my recipe for Lofty Lasagna, page 161.)
- Slice and layer in sandwiches. Use any sandwich spread you like—such as hummus or nut cheese—and add some crunchy vegetables along with the taters. It's great!
- Make open-face sandwiches with sliced potatoes, season the tops, and place under the broiler until toasty.
- Grill cooked white potato slices! They are amazing. Sweet potatoes won't hold up well on the grill when precooked, but you can grill them from uncooked (in thin slices).

Grains

Use precooked or leftover rice, quinoa, millet, and other grains in some of these ways:

- Add to burger patty mixtures. Make some in this book, or find other reliable recipes that use them. Once you have the hang of making burger recipes, you can begin to customize with your own mix of beans, seeds/nuts, vegetables, grains, and seasonings.
- Use as a base for soups and stews: This is one of my favorite ways to use prepped grains. It's like a Buddha bowl but uses a soup or stew as the topping for your base grain. A thick soup works particularly well, whether homemade or store-bought. Reheat your grain and put a scoop in a bowl, then top with soup, stew, or chili. Or, pack the grain into one side of the bowl (like a half-moon shape) and fill the other half with your stew. This not only makes the soup more nutritious, but also helps spread it over more people for a meal.
- Make a quick stir-fry or pilaf. Much like my Quinoa-Lentil Stir-Fry (page 183), you can use any leftover grain to work into a sauce of onions, veggies, and whatever seasonings you like. This kind of meal comes together very quickly.
- Use in tortilla wraps. Spread a layer of the grain (warm or cold) on your tortilla, then layer on other favorites. Add a sauce, spread, or simple salsa. Fold or roll it up and you have a fast lunch wrap.
- Make a quick Buddha bowl with any ingredients you have on hand. Add greens, some chopped veg, diced avocado, a dressing—boom, you're done!

Beans

Many of the ideas for grains apply equally well for beans, so review the grains ideas above. Here are some additional ideas:

- Add to soups and stews to bulk them up. As with grains, this adds nutrient density and helps spread the soup over more people.
- Mix into pasta sauce for a heartier pasta meal.
- Mix into salsa! Use to top grains or potatoes, or enjoy on taco night.
- Mash with avocado and seasonings for a sandwich filling.

- Chop beans to change their size and texture and add to a chili or taco mix.
- Source international vegan sauces (for example, Thai sauces, Indian curry sauces, enchilada sauces) and mix with beans, warm in an ovenproof dish, and serve over grains or greens.
- Think outside the standard hummus. Make bean purees with other varieties of beans and different seasoning blends. I have many recipes for inspiration on my website and in my other books. Once you get the hang of proportions, you won't need a recipe!
- Mash with seasonings and condiments for a sandwich filling. Add diced vegetables, pickles, olives, or any flavor elements you like. Layer between bread with lettuce, sliced avocado, or any other fixings.
- Top store-bought vegan pizzas. Why not? Sprinkle on chickpeas, maybe add extra veggies, too, to make it more nutritious and filling.

Croutons and Breadcrumbs

It's a familiar sight in my fridge: several bags of bread with a couple of heels or one stale slice. Instead of composting:

- Transform those unwanted pieces into croutons for your next salad (see my recipe for Bread-End Croutons, page 77).
- Turn them into breadcrumbs. Breadcrumbs freeze so well, and since it's almost impossible to find whole-grain breadcrumbs, you may as well make your own! Take those bread scraps and whiz in a food processor until crumbly.

Or, save the processing until you have collected enough random bread pieces in a freezer bag. Thaw or partially thaw to add to your processor. Whiz until crumbly, then use or pop back in the freezer. Breadcrumbs are then at your fingertips to use in stuffings or to top casseroles.

Refrigerated Coconut Milk and Coconut Cream

You'll notice some recipes call for coconut cream (from refrigerated canned coconut milk). This thick cream rises to the top of a can of coconut milk when it's chilled. I recommend you keep a can or two of coconut milk in your fridge so that if you are inspired with a recipe, it's waiting for you!

But don't get rid of the thin liquid, either. (Sometimes we refrigerate this for a few days … until we forget about it and it goes bad!) If you are organized, you can freeze the leftover liquid, then thaw it to use in soups or smoothies, or even for sautéing.

BEFORE YOU START COOKING . . .

Always review and read the recipe. We've all been there: in a smooth groove with a recipe only to discover you don't have the ingredient or tool you need for the job. If you take a few minutes to review the ingredients—and the directions—you'll set yourself up for success, and also more confidence and ease in the kitchen.

3
Kind Kitchen FAQs

Everything You Want to Know About Using Ingredients and Substitutions

In my early days of cooking, I learned by researching ingredients online and in books, watching some great cooking shows that talked about cooking techniques and foods, and plenty of practice. Like anything we do in life, we refine and grow through daily practice. Still, I think we can soften your learning curve in general cooking, and also in using my recipes.

In the many years of posting recipes online, and answering questions by way of email and also in cooking demos, certain questions repeatedly come up. You have probably asked yourself many of these—or will once you move into the recipe section of this book. So, let's cover those questions right now! Before you hit the recipes, or if you are new to plant-based cooking, take a few minutes to review these FAQs.

ALL ABOUT INGREDIENTS AND SUBSTITUTIONS

What is the difference between silken tofu and regular tofu? And medium tofu and extra-firm tofu? It's confusing!

Yes, tofu can be confusing and even intimidating if you haven't worked with it very often. I have heard from readers who tried to make frosting with extra-firm tofu or a stir-fry with soft tofu. Both not so successful! Regular (non-silken) tofu comes in soft, medium, firm, and extra-firm textures. Firm and extra-firm tofu are best for stir-fries, and slicing, cubing, or crumbling for those "meaty" textures. The softer varieties work well for scrambles and to use as dairy replacements in certain dishes.

With silken tofu, it doesn't matter if it's soft, firm, or extra-firm: It is almost always used in a puree of some sort—for things like puddings, creams, sauces, and pies—so use silken only in recipes that specifically call for it. Don't use it for stir-fries or marinating (even if the package says you can!).

Tofu packaging also varies. The regular varieties most often come in plastic packaging of some type; silken tofu comes in aseptic shelf-stable boxes. Since silken tofu does not need to be refrigerated, you might find it stocked on shelves in some stores or with the refrigerated tofu in other stores (which makes it *more* confusing)! Once you have opened a package of tofu, store it in an airtight container in the fridge for up to 6 days.

Why do some of your recipes specify red or Yukon Gold potatoes? Can't I use russet?

When I was learning to cook, I didn't know the differences between varieties of potatoes. Yukon Gold and red potatoes are considered waxy or lower-starch potatoes. These potatoes hold their shape and consistency when cooked, and so are best for salads, boiling, and roasting. Russet potatoes are starchy potatoes. They are most often used for baked potatoes and mashed potatoes. I find the flavor of red and yellow potatoes a little sweeter and more interesting than russet potatoes, so I tend to use them most of the time.

Can I substitute dried herbs for fresh herbs?

Sometimes, but not always. There are certain recipes for which dried herbs cannot be used as a substitution because the fresh herb is the foundation of the recipe—as with pesto. I try to specify in recipes when the substitution is okay. In general, dried herbs are used in dishes like soups, stews, and casseroles when they can be added in the earlier stages so that the flavors will be drawn out through the cooking time. Fresh herbs should be added toward the end of cooking a dish to finish it—the brief cooking just pops the flavor. This is especially true for leafy herbs like basil, parsley, cilantro, and dill, which should be added to a dish just a few minutes before serving. Hardier herbs like rosemary, oregano, and thyme fare better with more prolonged cooking. When you want to substitute dried for fresh herbs, a good guideline is to use roughly a quarter to a third of the dried to replace the fresh. For instance, use 1 teaspoon of a dried herb to replace 1 tablespoon of fresh.

Why do your recipes specify chickpea miso? What if I can't get that?

After discovering chickpea miso several years ago, I can't get enough of it! The flavor is quite mild, yet it adds that umami quality to recipes. Also, it offers an alternative for people with soy sensitivities. There are a few brands available now, but if you cannot find one, substitute a light/mellow soy-based miso.

Can I substitute cornstarch in your recipes that call for arrowroot?

I keep arrowroot on hand as it can be heated longer (and reheated) without breaking down, and it freezes and thaws more successfully in sauces than cornstarch. Also, arrowroot works better than cornstarch when thickening a sauce with acid (such as citrus juice). But in most cases they are good swaps for one another, and cornstarch can be substituted measure-for-measure for arrowroot.

What can you substitute for nutritional yeast?

There truly isn't an easy substitute for nutritional yeast. It is one of those unique ingredients. If the recipe requires only a small amount—a tablespoon or less—I'd say you can easily omit it. However, if the recipe requires an appreciable amount of nutritional yeast (several tablespoons or more), then you probably shouldn't make the recipe without it. Source the nutritional yeast and then get cooking!

What is the best plant-based milk to use in cooking and baking?

While personal preference always comes into play here, I have always preferred unsweetened organic soy milk for cooking, and more recently unsweetened oat milk for cooking. For baking, soy milks again almost always work well. I also quite like oat milk and nut milks for baking. Do check my notes; sometimes homemade oat milk can impart a sticky quality to dishes.

Can I substitute white beans for cashews to make a dish lower-fat?

This question comes up often online, when I've shared a recipe that uses pureed cashews for a creamy texture, such as in dips, cheeses, spreads, and sauces. You can likely replace up to about a quarter or a third of the total amount of cashews with white beans. Any more than that will really change the texture, quality, and taste of the final dish. My advice is, if you want to experiment, first make the recipe as is. Then, after tasting the dish as it is designed, you can play with substitutions next time around.

You substitute seeds for nuts in some recipes. What can I substitute for cashews? Can I substitute seeds for nuts all the time?

Seeds and nuts have different flavor profiles. Seeds are naturally more bitter than nuts. I have tried to offer nut-free alternatives in most recipes. In most cases, you can substitute sunflower seeds for cashews, with the caveat that you should use less (because they more densely fill a measure) and you may need to tweak the seasonings to sweeten slightly (they are naturally more bitter). Sometimes I use a combination of sunflower seeds and shredded coconut, or sunflower seeds and pumpkin seeds. It truly depends on the recipe.

Are hemp seeds the same things as hemp seed hearts?

Yes. Hemp seeds are sold after shelling, so sometimes they are called the hearts of hemp seeds.

Is there something I can substitute for refrigerated canned coconut cream? I can't consume coconut milk.

You'll notice that some recipes call for coconut cream (from refrigerated canned coconut milk); see my note about this on page 15. If you can't have coconut, try a rich-tasting nondairy creamer (opt for plain) or Cashew Cream (page 115). They won't work in every recipe, but they're your best options.

I can't consume vinegar; what can I substitute?

If you can use lemon or lime juice, they will work in some of the recipes—there are always some flavor differences, of course, but citrus is acidic like vinegar.

What's the best egg replacer?

It depends. I haven't ever baked with a powdered egg replacer. I don't think it's necessary. And you don't always need to "replace" an egg in a recipe. Sometimes it's a matter of extra binding or some leavening, but the ingredients in any given recipe might already offer those things for you.

It also depends on whether it's needed for baking or for cooking. For instance, in baking we can leaven with baking powder, and also baking soda combined with an acidic element such as lemon juice or vinegar. For stability and binding, this can come from pureed bananas, nut butter, nondairy yogurt, or ground flax mixed with water. It's not a one-size-fits-all type of thing. But I'll say this: I find plant-based baking easier than traditional baking. There's no need to cream butter with sugar, and no need to separate eggs. So, relax and have fun with the recipes. Over time you'll get a sense of what works well for binding and leavening if you want to modify your own family favorite recipes.

What's the difference between almond meal and almond flour?

There's no difference; almond meal is simply whole almonds processed into a fine meal. It's used in baking and so sometimes called almond flour.

How do I make your baking recipes gluten-free? Can I substitute coconut flour for regular flour?

If the recipe isn't naturally gluten-free or oat-based (where you can use a certified gluten-free flour), it is best to source a reputable all-purpose gluten-free flour mix and experiment with one of those. I'm often asked about coconut flour, in particular; it's quite an unusual flour. It's more "thirsty" than regular flours, meaning it soaks up more of the liquid in the recipe. Unless you are familiar working with coconut flour and know what is required to modify recipes when using it, I wouldn't recommend using it as a substitute.

Why do you use spelt flour? Can't I use whole-wheat flour?

While spelt flour isn't gluten-free, it can often be tolerated by people who cannot consume traditional wheat flour. I started baking with it about 15 years ago, and found that I really loved the fresher flavor and texture it offered for baked goods. It mixes more easily with less stickiness and clumping. I still use whole-wheat flour, but most often white wheat flour and whole-wheat pastry flour.

White wheat flour is not refined flour. It's a whole-grain flour that is made from a different variety of wheat, so it is very light in color and texture. It's wonderful to use in cakes and other baked goods. If my recipe calls for spelt flour and you want to substitute whole-wheat pastry flour, use this conversion: for every 1 cup of spelt flour, use a scant cup of whole-wheat pastry flour (about 1 cup less 1–2 tablespoons).

Can I substitute dates for sugar or maple syrup in the recipe?

Dates are a wonderful option to sweeten recipes naturally. They don't always substitute well for granulated sugar in recipes, however. If a recipe calls for coconut sugar, you can typically substitute date sugar with good results (they aren't exactly alike but it's a fair substitute). The trouble with substituting dates for a granulated sugar—or a liquid sweetener—is that the texture is quite different. The recipe will require other modifications for texture. So stick with the same texture sweetener substitutes for best results.

Can I substitute applesauce for nuts/seeds/nut butters in baking to make it lower-fat?

The answer is similar to the white beans question on page 19, except that with baking, there are more factors to consider. For cookies, you need a whole-foods fat for texture (such as nut butter). If you use applesauce, you will instead get a muffin-like texture. (Which is fine if you want muffins—but not if you want cookies!) For muffins and quick breads, you can indeed use applesauce in order to reduce fat, but it tends to make all baked goods taste the same. And I don't think applesauce is a good option for chocolate muffins or cake. There are other options for lower-fat baking beyond applesauce, as you will see in these recipes!

Can I substitute cocoa nibs for chocolate chips?

These are very different ingredients, so I don't recommend it. Cocoa nibs are very hard and bitter. Try tasting a few cocoa nibs straight up first before using them: Chew, and you'll see how very different they are in taste and texture. Then you can decide.

Is all dark chocolate vegan?

No, so it is very important to read labels and ingredient lists. Most dark chocolate (70 percent cacao and over) is dairy-free, but some kinds contain traces of milk fat or other dairy-based ingredients. Also, there are some brands of vegan chocolate that are easily identifiable as vegan, but they don't taste as good as other dark chocolate bars. Do some sampling, and search for reviews of great dark chocolate.

Is there any such thing as oil-free chocolate?

Through a Facebook group I heard about a brand called Nibble Chocolate that is made with just two ingredients: cocoa beans and whole unrefined cane sugar. It's beautiful chocolate and you can purchase it online. I do use other dark chocolate in my baking (mostly for convenience), but this is an option I can confidently recommend.

Why do some of your recipes specify vanilla bean powder?

Vanilla bean powder is the whole vanilla bean ground into powder. It has an exquisite flavor and aroma. It's a little pricey, but a little goes a very long way! In recipes where vanilla extract can be substituted, I have noted that in the ingredients. If the substitution isn't listed, simply omit from the recipe.

ALL ABOUT TECHNIQUES

How do I sauté without oil?

I will guide you through my technique for sautéing onions and other veggies in recipes where it's required, but here are some useful tips.

First, start with a good-quality nonstick pan. Today's nonstick pans are not the ones of a decade back. There are higher-quality pans made with more healthful and environmentally friendly materials. Invest in one or two good pans before you get cooking!

Next, consider the vegetables you are using:

Mushrooms will release a lot of water, so you can dry sauté them with spices. Don't add any liquid when beginning to sauté, just let the heat do its job, and as the mushrooms reduce and begin to brown, then you can add some tamari and/or balsamic vinegar for flavor. The mushrooms will absorb the flavors and continue to brown.

Harder vegetables like broccoli, cauliflower, carrots, and green beans need some steaming of sorts. It's useful to cover the pan and cook over medium heat with a splash of liquid (broth or water) to allow the vegetables to slowly steam in that enclosed heat, stirring occasionally. Then, once they have just become tender, you can bump the heat to high and add some sauce or seasonings to bring a sear to the vegetables. Or, serve as they are, perfectly steamed with a little seasoning.

Vegetables like zucchini, onions, and bell peppers that are "in between" mushrooms and those hard vegetables need a little coaxing with liquid to get cooking, but not too much. Begin to sauté with a couple teaspoons of liquid, and as it evaporates, add a little more. The idea is to add enough to keep the vegetables from sticking but not so much that it makes the vegetables soggy. To caramelize vegetables such as onions and bell peppers, continue cooking over high heat, adding a few pinches of salt and just a small amount of liquid as you go. Start with a tablespoon or so, and as it evaporates, add a little bit more. I like to add a little red or white wine, or balsamic reduction to enhance the caramelization. If the vegetables are sticking, again add a teaspoon or two of water to loosen the juices on the pan, and continue. You may need to do this deglazing several times. This is where all the flavor is, so bring those flavors back into the vegetables! The caramelization process will take a little longer than a simple sauté, so give it time.

Garlic has a tendency to burn easily. Be sure to begin sautéing other vegetables first and then add the garlic toward the end of cooking when there is more moisture in the pan, and keep the heat at medium so as not to burn the garlic. If the garlic burns, it becomes very bitter and will ruin the overall flavor.

I thought these recipes were oil-free! Do I really need to lightly oil a dish for baking?
When I note to lightly wipe with oil, I mean to literally dab a paper towel with oil and wipe the inner surface of the dish. If baking with glass or other dishes that tend to stick, this is very helpful and the amount of oil is negligible. I opt to do the light-wipe and also line with parchment paper so you can easily remove the baked goods after baking. If you have a very good nonstick pan, you may be able to skip the wipe of oil.

Do I need to use paper liners for muffins? Why are my muffins sticking to the liners?
If you don't use muffin liners, you will need to oil or spray your muffin pan before filling. I find this method unreliable, as sometimes the muffins still stick. Also, cleaning is tedious! Muffin liners solve this problem. However, many paper liners don't easily peel away from the baked muffin. The best choice is parchment liners. Muffins and cupcakes turn out beautifully when using them, and they will not stick.

Why do you soak nuts for recipes? How long does it take to soak nuts?
Not all recipes require nuts to be soaked. When a recipe calls for soaked nuts, it's so the nuts will puree smoothly with blending. Rather than soaking nuts in small amounts for one or another recipe, it's helpful to prepare them in batches so you have them at the ready in your freezer. For instance, rather than soaking ½ cup of almonds or cashews for a recipe, batch-soak larger portions (4–5 cups). See the Batch-Cooking section (page 12) for directions on soaking and storing nuts.

Why do you roast nuts and seeds? And what's the best way to roast them?
Toasting nuts and seeds enhances their flavor. In addition, if fat content is a concern for you, toasting nuts is helpful because you get more intense flavor and can therefore use a smaller amount in a recipe. Roasting or toasting nuts and seeds is simple, but you do need to be attentive as they are roasting. Some chefs dry-roast in a pan. I prefer to use my toaster oven. See the Batch-Cooking section (page 13) for directions on how to roast nuts and seeds.

How do you melt chocolate? Sometimes it burns or seizes when I melt it.

Since chocolate burns easily, it's best not to melt it with direct heat from the stove or in the microwave. Instead, put the chocolate in a heatproof bowl or small saucepan over a larger saucepan of gently simmering water; the bowl should rest on the rim of the saucepan and not touch the water below. The heat from the simmering water will melt the chocolate slowly and more evenly. Be careful not to drop *any* water into the melting chocolate. Even a drop of water will make the chocolate seize up and become difficult to work with.

ALL ABOUT STORAGE

Can I freeze your burger recipes?

Yes! To freeze, prepare the batch of burger mix, then shape the patties. Layer the uncooked patties separated with slips of parchment paper in an airtight container. Place in the freezer for up to 4 months. To cook, allow the patties to thaw at room temperature, then cook as per the recipe directions.

Do I need to refrigerate flax seeds and hemp seeds? What about flax meal?

Both flax seeds and hemp seeds are shelf-stable. Flax meal, however, does need to be kept refrigerated or frozen. It can be used straight from frozen, which makes it very convenient for recipes.

Do nuts need to be stored in the freezer?

If you buy nuts in large quantities and they are being stored over the course of many months or a year, you should refrigerate or freeze them. Softer nuts like walnuts and pecans can go rancid in warmer months when stored in the cupboard.

I can freeze hummus?

Yes! This answer seems to surprise people. Hummus freezes very well. When I make hummus, I make a double or triple batch. That way I can portion extra in airtight containers and freeze. Thaw at room temperature overnight to enjoy the next day, or allow the container to sit in a warm water bath for a few hours to hasten thawing.

Okay, if I can freeze hummus, can I freeze nut cheeses?

Also yes! Follow the same procedure as with hummus.

Can I leave baked goods like muffins and cookies out on the counter or do I need to refrigerate?

I always refrigerate, especially for muffins and quick breads, as they are more perishable. Since they don't have any preservatives, muffins and baked goods can become moldy after a couple of days at room temperature, especially during warm months. So, pop them in the fridge! If you want that "freshly baked" vibe, gently reheat in a very low oven or toaster oven for 5–10 minutes.

Can cakes and cupcakes be frozen?

Most of the time, yes. Be sure they are fully cooled, then store in a sturdy airtight container in the freezer for up to 2 months. While you can freeze for longer, the taste does become a bit freezer-burned after a couple of months. You can also freeze a cooled cake and its frosting separately and then frost after thawing.

What do I do with leftover canned coconut milk?

An open can of coconut milk can be kept in the fridge for up to 6 days. I like to transfer the contents to a jar with a tight lid. If you aren't sure about freshness after a few days, take a sniff—when in doubt, throw it out. However, if you don't expect to use the opened coconut milk within the week, freeze it in an airtight container (or in measured portions, such as 1 tablespoon or 2 tablespoons). Be sure to freeze the thick cream separate from the watery liquid.

What is aquafaba and how is it stored?

Aquafaba means "bean water." It is the liquid drained from a can of beans, preferably chickpeas or white beans. Aquafaba is useful as an egg white replacer in many recipes. When opening a can of chickpeas or white beans, drain over a bowl to catch the bean water. Then, use in recipes as directed. Often you will have extra aquafaba, which can be stored in an airtight container in the fridge for up to 3-4 days, or in the freezer for a couple of months.

PART TWO

The Recipes

4
Breakfast Vibes

Be kind to yourself and start your day with a nourishing breakfast!
Here you'll find a great variety of whole-grain and oil-free muffins and
baked goods, cereals, pancakes and waffles, scramble and "eggs," and
the most delicious next-level avocado toast. Not a breakfast person?
This chapter still is not to be missed; most of these recipes can be
enjoyed as a lunch, afternoon nosh—or even a nighttime snack!

Dreena's Morning Green Smoothie

I've been enjoying green smoothies for many years now. They aren't as "in fashion" as they once were, and now many recipes and prepared smoothies include a lot of fruit, making them high in sugar. I like my smoothies quite green—more like a green drink some days—and with a good dose of lemon and ginger. The bitter notes in greens become more "friendly" to our taste buds over time, so you get used to having less fruit in your smoothies! I often start making mine with less fruit than what's listed below, take my half of the batch, then blend a little more fruit with the remaining smoothie for any family members who want theirs sweeter. This recipe is very flexible. Adjust and taste as you go.

Serves 2–3; makes 3½–4 cups

2–2½ cups (packed) spinach leaves (see note)

½ cup fresh parsley (see note)

1 medium or ½ large lemon, peeled (see note)

1 orange, peeled (see note)

1 cup frozen pineapple chunks (see note)

½–⅔ cup sliced cucumber (peel and seeds intact)

1 tablespoon flax meal *or* 2 tablespoons hemp seeds

1–2 Brazil nuts (optional)

1 tablespoon grated fresh ginger (peeling optional)

½–1 cup water

Starting with ½ cup water, put all the ingredients in a blender. Puree for a minute or more, until the smoothie reaches your desired consistency, adding extra water if needed to blend or for thinner smoothies. Taste, and adjust with additional fruit or other add-ins as desired. Pour into glasses and serve.

Spinach Note: Other greens can be substituted here. I most often rotate between spinach and kale. Kale has a much stronger flavor, so when I use it, I use somewhat less and sub in more cucumber or parsley to add up to 2½ cups. If you have trouble adjusting to the flavor of kale or other greens in the smoothie, trying adding more pineapple. It really helps mask the taste of kale and collards!

Parsley Note: I always add fresh parsley to my green smoothies. It's abundant in vitamin K and a good source of iron and calcium. Rinse it well before using and remove and discard any thick, coarse stems. Keep in the fridge for up to a week to use in your smoothies.

Lemon Note: Add a little lemon (or lime) to a green smoothie and you'll never want to go without it! The bright tang really picks up the flavor of the smoothie. I try to use organic whenever I can. To use lemon in this smoothie, trim away most of the peel but leave the white pith intact (it's full of nutrients). I also don't remove the seeds—just let the blender do its work on those!

Orange Note: Instead of an orange, try 2 or 3 peeled mandarins or 1 cored apple.

Pineapple Note: Frozen mango chunks or frozen sliced bananas make a tasty substitution for the pineapple!

Oat+ Milk

Oat milk is one of the most beloved plant-based milks. It's also one of the easiest to make at home. Try this version, which has a little "extra" with the addition of pumpkin seeds. Note that this recipe is best served as a beverage. Commercial plant-based milks are smoother and generally work better for cooking.

Makes about 3 cups

3 tablespoons pumpkin seeds (see note)

2 pitted dates (optional; see note)

2 cups cold water, divided

1½–2 cups ice

½ cup rolled oats

¼ teaspoon pure vanilla bean powder (optional)

Combine the pumpkin seeds, dates (if using), and 1 cup of the water in a blender. Puree for a minute or more, until fully blended. Then add the remaining 1 cup water, ice, and oats. Pulse several times or puree for about 10 seconds (see note). Use a funnel and fine strainer (or nut milk bag) to strain the milk. Don't squish or press the mixture. Simply allow the milk to drain through, then discard the pulp. If using the vanilla bean powder, stir it in. Pour into glasses and serve, or store in a covered jar in the refrigerator for up to 4 days.

Pumpkin Seed Note: Instead of pumpkin seeds, you can swap in hemp seeds or ¼ cup of raw cashews or almonds.

Date Note: You can omit the dates if you don't want a sweetened version—or add another couple of dates for a sweeter option.

Blending Note: Homemade oat milk becomes sticky, even a little slimy, if overprocessed. This is why we process the dates with the pumpkin seeds first, then pulse in the oats only briefly.

Pressure Cooker Pumpkin Steel-Cut Oats

The coziness of steel-cut oats pairs sweetly with pumpkin warmth. These oats are ready in a flash, and you can dig in to some fall goodness any time of the year!

Serves 4

1 cup steel-cut oats

¾ cup pumpkin puree (about half of a 15-ounce can)

⅓ cup chopped unsulfured dried apricots (see note)

½ teaspoon pumpkin pie spice

¼ teaspoon ground cinnamon

⅛ teaspoon pure vanilla bean powder (optional)

Pinch sea salt

2 cups water (see note)

1 cup vanilla or plain nondairy milk

1 teaspoon fresh lemon juice

Toppings (optional)

Pure maple syrup or coconut sugar

Pumpkin seeds

Chopped pecans or walnuts

Shredded coconut

Raisins

Put all the ingredients (except the optional toppings) in a multifunction pressure cooker (such as an Instant Pot). Stir to combine.

Secure the lid and set the valve to the "sealed" position. Press the Manual button, then set the cook time for 4 minutes at high pressure. Allow the pot to come to pressure and cook. Once the timer goes off, turn off the pot and allow the pressure to naturally release for 15 minutes. After 15 minutes, release the lid and stir the oatmeal. Add any additional seasonings to taste, if desired, and serve with your favorite toppings.

Apricot Note: I like using apricots here because they don't quite dull the vibrant orange color of the pumpkin the way dates or raisins do. You can certainly use dates or raisins, or omit the dried fruit altogether. You can also add a touch of dried fruit as a topping on the finished bowls.

Water Note: Using hot or boiling water helps speed up the time it takes for the Instant Pot to reach pressure and start cooking. You can use room-temperature or cold water; it will just take a little longer.

Wow 'em Waffles

Many people think waffles can't be tasty if they are vegan. Not so! These waffles have a gorgeous golden color, and are just lightly sweet with a crispy-tender texture. Time to wow 'em!

Makes 4 medium-large waffles

1 cup nondairy plain or vanilla yogurt

1 cup sliced ripe banana (see note)

1 cup oat flour

½ cup almond meal (see nut-free note)

1½ teaspoons baking powder

Pinch salt

2 teaspoons pure vanilla extract

Preheat your waffle maker according to the manufacturer's instructions.

Put the yogurt and banana in a blender (or in a deep cup if using an immersion blender) and blend until smooth. In a mixing bowl, stir together the oat flour, almond meal, baking powder, and salt. Add the yogurt-banana mixture to the dry ingredients along with the vanilla. Mix to combine fully.

When the waffle maker is ready, ladle about ½ cup of the batter into each waffle mold. Close the lid and let the waffle cook and set for 4½–5 minutes (the time will depend on the brand of waffle maker). Check at the end of this time, and if the waffles need a little more browning, allow them to cook for about another minute. When ready, remove and transfer to a cooling rack. Repeat with the remaining batter.

Banana Note: The banana doesn't have to be overripe, as when making banana bread, but it should be ripe enough to have natural sweetness. You'll need 2 small to medium bananas to yield 1 cup sliced bananas.

Nut-Free Note: For a nut-free version, replace the almond meal with a mix of ¼ cup pumpkin seed meal plus ¼ cup hemp seeds.

Serving Suggestions: These waffles are tasty straight up because they are lightly sweetened with the banana and vanilla. Try serving with fresh fruit and a drizzle of maple syrup, and maybe a dollop of vegan whipped cream—or, better yet, with a big spoonful of Dessert Cashew Cream (page 246) or Coconut-Date Caramel Cream (page 247).

Next-Level Avocado Toast

Avocado toast gets elevated in this recipe. Skeptical about the miso and sweet potato? So were my kids—and my recipe testers—before trying it. But the contrast of the salty, umami miso with the sweet layer of potato and richness of avocado is quite divine!

Serves 1–2

2 slices whole-grain bread

2 teaspoons chickpea miso or other mild miso

½ cup mashed cooked sweet potato flesh (optionally warmed; see note)

Few pinches smoked paprika (optional)

Couple pinches sea salt

1 teaspoon fresh lemon juice

½–¾ cup sliced ripe avocado (see note)

Freshly ground black pepper to taste (optional)

Toast the bread as much as desired. While the bread is still warm, spread 1 teaspoon of the miso on each slice. Add the sweet potato, smoked paprika (if using), and a pinch of salt. Sprinkle the lemon juice over the avocado slices, then place those over the sweet potato layer. Add another sprinkle of salt and a few grinds of pepper to taste if you like.

Sweet Potato Note: Bake the spuds in advance! Place whole sweet potatoes on a rimmed baking sheet lined with parchment paper. Bake at 425°F for 40–50 minutes, until fully tender, then scoop the flesh into a bowl and mash. Store in an airtight container in the fridge for up to 6 days or in the freezer for a couple of months. You can use it on these avocado toasts straight from the fridge, or reheat to just warm it through.

Avocado Note: If you don't have a ripe avocado on hand, try instead using a thin layer of tahini on top of the miso (1–1½ teaspoons for each slice) and then top with the sweet potato.

Potato-Cauliflower Scramble

The cauliflower in this tasty scramble is easily camouflaged by the spuds and tofu (if you're in need of "sneaking" it in)! This dish is equally satisfying for lunch or dinner.

Serves 3–4

2–4 tablespoons water

½ cup chopped green onions *or* 3 tablespoons dried onion flakes

1 cup finely chopped zucchini

2½–3 cups steamed cauliflower florets, mashed (see note)

1 (12–16-ounce) package medium or firm tofu, drained and crumbled

2 cups chopped cooked potato (see note)

1 teaspoon Dijon mustard

½ teaspoon garlic powder

¼ teaspoon salt, or more to taste

Freshly ground black pepper to taste (optional)

2½ tablespoons nutritional yeast

2 tablespoons tahini

½–¾ teaspoon black salt (see note)

2–3 cups chopped spinach or kale (optional)

Heat a large nonstick skillet over medium-high heat. Pour in 2 tablespoons water and add the onions and zucchini. Cook for 5 minutes, or until slightly softened, then add the cauliflower, tofu, potato, mustard, garlic powder, salt, and pepper (if desired). Cook for 3–4 minutes, then add the nutritional yeast and tahini and stir to combine. If the mixture is sticking to the pan, add another tablespoon or two of water. To finish, add the black salt; if you're using greens, add them and stir until just wilted and still bright green (spinach will cook faster than kale). Season to taste with extra salt, pepper, and black salt, and serve.

Cauliflower Note: Steaming the cauliflower helps it break down nicely in this scramble. You can steam it a day or two ahead of time to help speed preparation and store it in an airtight container in the fridge.

Potato Note: I prefer using cooked waxy potatoes here, but russets can be used if you have them on hand. (Check out the batch-cooking directions on page 11.) If you don't have cooked potatoes handy, try grating raw potatoes, and add them to the pan with the onion and zucchini; you'll need to add extra water to prevent sticking.

Black Salt Note: Also known as kala namak, black salt is not actually black but rather a light pink. Added just when finishing a dish, it contributes an eggy flavor to the scramble (that flavor dissipates with cooking). If you don't have it, simply season with an additional ½–¾ teaspoon salt to taste.

Ideas: For other add-ins, try ½ cup chopped fresh tomato, 2–3 tablespoons chopped sun-dried tomatoes, 1–2 tablespoons sliced pitted olives, and/or a splash of hot sauce.

Mother Nature's Muesli

Muesli is one of the easiest things you can make. It is similar to overnight oats—but as it was created decades back, it never got the internet attention! Unlike overnight oats, muesli typically includes more seeds, nuts, and dried fruit. I have created this muesli to be nut-free, but feel free to modify with your favorite nuts and other ingredients (see notes). The recipe is very flexible!

Serves 4

2 cups rolled oats

¼ cup hemp seeds

¼ cup pumpkin or sunflower seeds (see note)

⅓–¾ cup chopped dried fruit (see note)

2 tablespoons unsweetened shredded coconut or additional seeds

¼ teaspoon ground cinnamon

Couple pinches ground nutmeg

Pinch sea salt

3½ cups vanilla nondairy milk, plus more for serving if desired

1 medium-large apple, cored and grated (see note)

Combine all the ingredients in a large bowl and stir well. (If you plan to soak the muesli overnight, you can hold off adding the apple until the morning, to keep it crisp and fresh.) Cover the bowl tightly and refrigerate for at least 2 hours or up to overnight.

After soaking, stir in extra milk to moisten as desired, and add the apple now if you left it out. Serve, topping with extra fruit if you like (see serving ideas).

Seed Note: If you like, put the pumpkin seeds (or both pumpkin and sunflower) in a mini food processor or blender and pulse just briefly to break them up. Also, if you don't have nut allergies, you can add chopped raw nuts like pistachios, walnuts, pecans, almonds, or hazelnuts.

Dried Fruit Note: There are so many options for dried fruit in this recipe! The most common dried fruits are raisins, cranberries, chopped dates, and chopped apricots. If you are able to source other dried fruits like organic peaches, mangoes, berries, or papayas, you can also use these in the muesli. With dried fruits like peaches, mangoes, and papayas, kitchen shears are useful to cut them into small pieces, rather than try to slice with a knife.

Apple Note: You can use any apple variety you love. Certain varieties oxidize less, including Gala, Cameo, and Ambrosia. These are great options if you want to add them to the muesli the night before.

Serving Suggestions:

- Top portions of muesli with seasonal fresh fruit, like berries and stone fruits in the summer, and chopped apples or pears or sliced grapes in the fall and winter.
- Top with a dollop of vanilla or other nondairy yogurt.
- If using a vanilla nondairy milk, you may find the muesli sweet enough, especially if using a more generous amount of dried fruit. Taste the mixture before serving, and if you feel it needs a bump of sweetness, sprinkle on some coconut or date sugar, or a drizzle of maple syrup.

Gingerbread Granola

This recipe brings the beauty and aroma of freshly baked gingerbread into a granola that is wonderful for breakfast or snacking. You can eat it straight or with nondairy milk, or top it with fresh fruit or nondairy yogurt. It's also perfect during the holidays—I make a batch for gifting every year!

Makes about 4½ cups

3 cups rolled oats

⅓–½ cup chopped pecans (see note for nut-free)

1½ teaspoons ground cinnamon

1 teaspoon ground ginger

¾ teaspoon ground allspice

⅛ teaspoon ground cloves

¼ teaspoon sea salt

3 tablespoons cashew butter or almond butter

2–4 tablespoons pure maple syrup

1½ teaspoons blackstrap molasses

¼ cup thick coconut nectar or date syrup (see note)

1 teaspoon pure vanilla extract

¼ cup dried cranberries or other dried fruit (optional; see note)

Preheat the oven to 300°F. Line a rimmed baking sheet with parchment paper.

In a large bowl, combine the oats, pecans, spices, and salt. In another bowl, combine the nut butter, maple syrup, and molasses, stirring to fully blend. Add the coconut nectar and vanilla to the nut butter mixture and stir well. Add the wet mixture to the dry and stir until well combined.

Transfer the mixture to the prepared baking sheet and spread out to evenly distribute. Bake for 27–30 minutes, stirring a couple of times to ensure the mixture browns evenly. Remove from the oven, stir in the dried fruit (if using) and bake for another 2–3 minutes. At this point the granola may not look completely dry, but do not overbake it, as it will dry more as it cools. Let cool completely, then break up into clusters. Once cool, store in an airtight container at room temperature for up to a month.

Nut-Free Note: Feel free to substitute 3–4 tablespoons pumpkin or sunflower seeds, or ¼ cup hemp seeds, in place of the nuts.

Coconut Nectar Note: This granola needs a thick sweetener to bind it together. The consistency should be similar to brown rice syrup or corn syrup. If you use a thinner sweetener, it won't hold together as well.

Dried Fruit Note: I don't always add dried fruit to granola, as I sometimes like the sweetness as is. So, you can choose to add some or not—and you can also try adding a few tablespoons of finely chopped crystallized ginger instead of cranberries or raisins for a definite flavor kick!

Spice Swap: For a more "everyday" version of this granola, omit the ginger, allspice, and cloves. Reduce the cinnamon to about 1 teaspoon, and add a few pinches of freshly grated nutmeg if you like. Also reduce the blackstrap molasses to 1–2 teaspoons.

Silky-Smooth Applesauce

Bursting with real apple flavor, this applesauce is far better than store-bought. Plus, with the help of an immersion blender, the texture becomes blissfully smooth!

Makes 5–6 cups

3 pounds medium apples (see note)

2–3 teaspoons fresh lemon juice

Add-Ins (optional)

¼–½ teaspoon ground cinnamon (see note)

¼ teaspoon pure vanilla bean powder

Pinch salt

3–4 tablespoons water (optional; see note)

1–2 pitted dates or a drizzle of pure maple syrup (optional; see note)

Core and roughly chop the apples, tossing with the lemon juice throughout chopping to help preserve color.

Put the chopped apples in a multifunction pressure cooker (such as an Instant Pot) with the lemon juice and any optional add-ins. Secure the lid and set the valve to the "sealed" position (see note). Press the Manual button, then set the cook time for 5 minutes at high pressure. Allow the pot to come to pressure and cook. Once the timer goes off, turn off the pot and allow the pressure to naturally release for 10–15 minutes. After 15 minutes, release the lid. Using an immersion blender, blend the mixture to your desired texture; you can leave it chunkier or fully puree it for a very smooth texture. Taste, and if you'd like a little sweetener or more cinnamon, adjust to taste. Remove the insert from the cooker to help speed cooling of the applesauce. Once fully cooled, transfer to jars or other airtight containers to refrigerate or freeze.

Apple Note: Peeling is optional! The peels make the applesauce slightly coarser and a little darker, but they don't change the flavor. If you're leaving the peels on, I do recommend organic apples. The variety of apple used will determine the sweetness of the applesauce. I use sweeter apples, such as Fuji and Gala, for my applesauce.

Cinnamon Note: The addition of cinnamon gives lovely flavor, but it does darken the applesauce a bit. It's up to you—you can omit it and then add just a touch after pureeing, adjusting to taste. A few pinches of grated nutmeg can also be added.

Water Note: I don't add water to my applesauce because I want to keep it quite thick. If your pressure cooker is prone to scorching without liquid, add this water with the apples.

Sweetener Note: Since you can never be sure how sweet the final applesauce will be, I recommend not adding any sweetener until after you've tasted it. (Because I choose sweeter apple varieties, I don't add any sweetener.) After cooking and pureeing, if you taste the applesauce and determine that you'd like it to be sweeter, stir in the maple syrup or place the dates in the hot applesauce to soak, then puree again once the dates have softened.

Idea: Switch up a portion of the apples for seasonal pears!

Sealing Ring: During one of my tests of this recipe, I accidentally used my standard sealing ring. Anyone who uses an Instant Pot knows that those sealing rings can hold a lot of odors. This particular time the sealing ring had held on to a lot of odor from the previous dish. My applesauce ended up having a faint oniony taste. It was unusable! Since that time, I have one designated sealing ring for "sweet" dishes and another for savory. Consider doing the same!

Stovetop Method: To make the applesauce on the stovetop, use the same ingredients, but add ¼ cup water. Combine all the ingredients except the optional sweetener in a large pot, cover, and place over medium heat. Allow the mixture to heat for a few minutes, then stir and cover again. If the mixture seems to be sticking, reduce the heat a little. Keep covered and let cook for 15–20 minutes, stirring occasionally for the first 5 minutes. Once the apples are fully tender, puree (adding sweetener if desired; see note), and allow to cool.

Top of the Muffin to You!

One morning I needed to bake a healthy snack and was short on time. I pulled out what I had on hand—a little cooked sweet potato, a ripe banana, and yogurt—and mixed it all with some flour to bake as muffin tops. They turned out so well that my youngest asked for them over and over. So the recipe began!

Makes 8–9 muffin tops

1 cup mix of sliced cooked yellow sweet potato flesh, cooled, and sliced ripe banana (see note)

1 tablespoon cashew butter or other nut butter

½ cup plain or vanilla nondairy yogurt (see note)

¼–⅓ cup pure maple syrup (see note)

1 cup oat flour

⅓ cup rolled oats

1½ teaspoons baking powder

½ teaspoon ground cinnamon

¼ teaspoon sea salt

Topping (optional)

1½ tablespoons rolled oats

1 tablespoon unrefined sugar

Preheat the oven to 350°F. Line a rimmed baking sheet with parchment paper.

In a mixing bowl, mash the sweet potato and banana together. Add the nut butter and mix, then mix in the yogurt and maple syrup. Add the flour, oats, baking powder, cinnamon, and salt. Stir until just combined.

Use a large spoon or ice cream scoop to place generous mounds of the batter on the prepared baking sheet, spaced a couple of inches apart. You should get 8 or 9 mounds. If using the topping, mix the oats and sugar together with your fingers in a cup or small bowl. Sprinkle over the top of the batter mounds. Bake for 18–19 minutes, until set to the touch. Remove and let them cool on the pan for a couple of minutes, then transfer to a wire rack to cool completely.

Potato/Banana Note: Any combination of sweet spuds and banana will do. Or, try all of one or the other! Using full sweet potato will be a little less sweet than including banana.

Yogurt Note: If using a vanilla nondairy yogurt, the batter will be sweeter. You can always reduce the maple syrup a little if you don't want them too sweet.

Maple Syrup Note: Adjust based on the sweetness of your yogurt. If using ¼ cup, make up the difference of liquid with about 1 tablespoon nondairy milk.

Lemon-Poppyseed Muffins

It was high time I created my own version for this classic muffin flavor. Tip: don't skip the topping!

Makes 12 muffins

2 cups oat flour

1 cup spelt flour

½ cup unrefined sugar (see note)

1–1½ tablespoons poppy seeds (see note)

2½ teaspoons baking powder

1–1½ teaspoon grated lemon zest

½ teaspoon baking soda

¼ teaspoons ground turmeric (optional)

¼ teaspoon (generous) sea salt

½ cup unsweetened applesauce

½ cup plain or vanilla nondairy yogurt (see note)

1 cup plain or vanilla nondairy milk (see note)

2 tablespoons pure maple syrup

1½ tablespoons fresh lemon juice

½–1 teaspoon pure lemon extract (optional; see note)

Topping

2 tablespoons unrefined sugar

1 tablespoon coconut butter

½ teaspoon grated lemon zest

Preheat the oven to 350°F. Line 12 cups of a muffin pan with parchment liners.

In a large bowl, combine the flours, sugar, poppy seeds, baking powder, lemon zest, baking soda, turmeric (if using), and salt. Stir to mix well. In another bowl, mix together the applesauce and yogurt, then stir in the milk, maple syrup, lemon juice, and lemon extract (if using). Add the wet mixture to the dry and stir until just combined.

Scoop the batter into the muffin liners. In a small bowl, combine the topping ingredients, crumbling them together with your fingers. Sprinkle the topping over the muffins.

Bake for 25–26 minutes, until the muffins are set and a toothpick or skewer inserted in the center comes out clean. Remove from the oven and cool for a couple of minutes in the pan, then transfer the muffins to a rack to cool completely.

Sugar Note: I typically use coconut sugar as a granulated sweetener. A lighter sugar such as unrefined cane sugar will result in a lighter color in the finished muffins. Which to use is up to you!

Poppy Seed Note: A mere 1½ tablespoons doesn't sound like a lot, but these tiny seeds spread out in the muffins as they bake. If you aren't sure how much poppy seed goodness you prefer, start with just 1 tablespoon.

Yogurt/Milk Note: If you use vanilla yogurt or milk, the muffins will be a touch sweeter, unless you can find unsweetened vanilla milk and yogurt.

Extract Note: The lemon zest alone contributes a good amount of lemon flavor to these muffins. But if you love a strong lemon essence and have pure lemon extract on hand, feel free to add some to complement it.

Sweet Potato Muffins

These tender, delicately spiced muffins are for all my fellow sweet potato lovers. After I posted this recipe on my blog, it quickly became a reader favorite!

Makes 12 muffins

1 cup cooked orange sweet potato flesh, cooled

2 tablespoons hemp seeds (see note)

1 cup nondairy milk

½ cup pure maple syrup

1 teaspoon pure vanilla extract

2 cups spelt flour *or* 2 cups less 2 tablespoons whole-wheat pastry flour

2 teaspoons baking powder

1½ teaspoons ground cinnamon

¼ teaspoon ground cardamom or nutmeg (optional)

¼ teaspoon baking soda

¼ teaspoon sea salt

¼ cup raisins or miniature nondairy chocolate chips, or a combination (optional)

Preheat the oven to 350°F. Line 12 cups of a muffin pan with parchment liners.

Combine the sweet potato, hemp seeds, milk, maple syrup, and vanilla in a blender and puree until very smooth. In a large bowl, stir together the flour, baking powder, cinnamon, cardamom (if using), baking soda, salt, and raisins and/or chocolate chips (if using). Stir until well combined. Add the wet mixture to the dry and stir until well combined.

Scoop the batter into the muffin liners. Bake for 24–26 minutes, until a toothpick inserted in the center comes out clean. Remove from the oven and cool for a couple of minutes in the pan, then transfer to a rack to cool more as desired.

Hemp Seed Note: The pureed hemp seeds add some fat to the muffin batter, so don't omit them. If you don't have them, you can use 2 tablespoons of another seed or chopped nut.

Chocolate Chip Muffins

When I was testing these muffins, they became a *fast* favorite in our home. As in . . . they disappeared fast! The banana is optional, but it adds an extra layer of flavor and delicate sweetness that's rather enchanting!

Makes 12 muffins

2 cups white wheat flour or whole-wheat pastry flour (see note)

1 cup almond meal

¼ cup coconut sugar

2 teaspoons baking powder

½ teaspoon baking soda

¼ teaspoon sea salt

1 cup plain or vanilla nondairy milk

⅓ cup pure maple syrup

2 teaspoons pure vanilla extract (see note)

½ cup diced ripe banana (optional)

½–¾ cup nondairy chocolate chips

Preheat the oven to 350°F. Line 12 cups of a muffin pan with parchment liners.

In a large bowl, combine the flour, almond meal, coconut sugar, baking powder, baking soda, and salt. In another bowl, combine the milk, maple syrup, and vanilla. Add the wet ingredients to the dry and stir until just combined (do not overmix). Gently fold in the banana (if using) and chocolate chips.

Scoop the batter into the prepared muffin liners and bake for 23 minutes, or until a toothpick inserted in the center comes out clean. Remove from the oven and let the muffins cool in the pan for a couple of minutes. Then, transfer the muffins to a rack to cool further.

Flour Note: White wheat flour is not all-purpose flour. It is a whole-grain flour that is made from a different variety of wheat, so it is very light in color and texture. It's wonderful to use in cakes and other baked goods and also in these muffins—it makes them extra fluffy! If you cannot find it in your store, whole-wheat pastry flour works just fine. If you want to substitute spelt flour, use a little more, about 2¼ cups in total.

Extract Note: If you love the flavor and aroma of almond extract, go ahead and include some here! Use just 1½ teaspoons vanilla and substitute the remaining ½ teaspoon with pure almond extract.

Hope's Blueberry Muffins

Fragrant with a pop of citrus, these tender blueberry muffins boast delicate crunchy-sweet tops. Whenever I bake these, our youngest daughter, Hope, runs for the cooling rack!

Makes 10–12 muffins

2½ cups spelt flour

½ cup unrefined sugar, plus 1–2 tablespoons for sprinkling

1 teaspoon baking powder

1 teaspoon baking soda

¼ teaspoon salt

1 teaspoon grated lemon or orange zest

1 cup plus 2 tablespoons plain or vanilla nondairy milk (see note)

½ cup plain or vanilla nondairy yogurt (see note)

1 tablespoon apple cider vinegar

1½ teaspoons pure vanilla extract

1 cup fresh or frozen blueberries, tossed in 1–2 teaspoons flour (see note)

Preheat the oven to 350°F. Line 10–12 cups of a muffin pan with parchment liners (see note).

In a large bowl, combine the flour, sugar, baking powder, baking soda, salt, and zest. In another bowl, combine about half of the milk with the yogurt, whisking to combine. Then, add the remaining milk, apple cider vinegar, and vanilla. Add the wet mixture to the dry, stirring well until just combined, then swiftly fold in the berries.

Scoop the mixture into the prepared muffin liners (see yield note). Sprinkle the 1–2 tablespoons sugar over top. Bake for 26–28 minutes (see berry note), until a toothpick or skewer inserted in the center comes out clean. Remove from the oven and cool for a couple of minutes in the pan, then transfer the muffins to a rack to finish cooling.

Milk/Yogurt Note: If you use vanilla milk or yogurt, the muffins will be a little sweeter, unless you can find unsweetened vanilla milk and yogurt.

Berry Note: When using frozen blueberries, the batter will take longer to set up, closer to 28 minutes, and there's always some "bleeding" of blue into the batter. (If you want to minimize this, you can first rinse the frozen berries until the water runs clear. Then, pat dry with towels and toss the berries in flour. I'm a little too impatient when baking to take that step— but it's a great option for aesthetics!) If using fresh berries, the muffins may be ready at 26 minutes. Finally, if you don't want the blueberries sinking to the bottom of the muffins, add a small amount of batter to each muffin liner before mixing in the berries. Then, add the berries to the batter and proceed with filling the cups! Note that you can also use raspberries or sliced/chopped strawberries.

Muffin Yield Note: Either fill 12 muffin cups for smaller muffins, or fill just 10–11 and have larger muffins—a little more like bakery-style! Larger muffins will take longer to bake through, so check them at 27–28 minutes, again keeping in mind that muffins with fresh berries will set a little sooner. Prefer mini muffins? Fill 24 cups (either nonstick or lined with parchment liners) and bake for 17–18 minutes.

Chocolate Zucchini Bread

Because the wet ingredients are mixed in a blender, you don't even need to grate the zucchini for this quick bread. And because it's chocolate, no one will know it has any zukes in it!

Makes 1 loaf or 12 muffins

1¾ cups whole-wheat pastry flour (see note)

½ cup cocoa powder

2 tablespoons coconut sugar

2 teaspoons baking powder

½ teaspoon baking soda

¼ teaspoon sea salt

2 cups thickly sliced zucchini

1 cup sliced very ripe bananas

¼ cup hemp seeds

⅔ cup pure maple syrup

¼ cup water

2 teaspoons pure vanilla extract

¼ cup nondairy chocolate chips

Preheat the oven to 350°F. Spray or wipe a loaf pan with a touch of oil and line with parchment paper, allowing some parchment to overhang the edges of the pan.

In a large bowl, stir together the flour, cocoa powder, coconut sugar, baking powder, baking soda, and salt.

Put the zucchini, bananas, hemp seeds, and maple syrup in a blender and puree until smooth. Once well pureed, add the water and vanilla and blend again.

Add the wet mixture to the dry and stir until just combined. Fold in the chocolate chips.

Pour the batter into the prepared pan. Bake for 50 minutes, or until a toothpick inserted in the center comes out clean. Remove from the oven and let the bread cool in the pan on a cooling rack. Once cool, remove the loaf from the pan by lifting the edges of the parchment. Peel the paper away from the loaf, then slice.

Flour Note: If you want to substitute spelt flour, use 2 cups.

Muffin Swap: If you want to make muffins instead of a quick bread, pour the batter into a 12-cup muffin pan lined with parchment liners and bake for 25 minutes, or until a toothpick inserted in the center comes out clean. Allow to cool in the pan for a few minutes, then transfer to a cooling rack to fully cool.

Light and Fluffy Pancakes

With just six ingredients, these are possibly the easiest pancakes I have ever made—simple enough to make any day of the week! Serve with pure maple syrup and fresh fruit, or try my Strawberry Sauce Forever (page 248) or Coconut-Date Caramel Cream (page 247).

Makes 10–11 small pancakes

1 cup plain or vanilla nondairy milk

1 tablespoon apple cider vinegar

1¼ cups white wheat flour or whole-wheat pastry flour (see note)

1 tablespoon baking powder

¼ teaspoon pure vanilla bean powder (optional; see note)

Couple pinches sea salt

In a small bowl, combine the milk and apple cider vinegar. Let sit for 5 minutes.

Heat a nonstick skillet (see note) over medium-high heat for a few minutes, then reduce the heat to medium.

While the pan is heating, in a large bowl, mix the flour, baking powder, vanilla bean powder (if using), and salt. Add the milk and vinegar mixture to the dry mixture and whisk to combine. Fold in any optional add-ins you like (see ideas).

Using a ladle, scoop ¼–⅓ cup of the batter into the hot pan, fitting as many as you can without allowing the pancakes to touch. Cook for several minutes, until small bubbles form on the outer edge and in the center and the pancakes starts to look dry on the top. Flip the pancakes and lightly cook the other side for about a minute, then transfer to a plate. Repeat until all the batter is used.

Flour Note: White wheat flour is not all-purpose flour. It is a whole-grain flour made from a different variety of wheat, so it is very light in color and texture. It's wonderful to use in these pancakes—makes them extra fluffy! If you cannot find it, whole-wheat pastry flour works just fine.

Vanilla Bean Powder Note: I love vanilla bean powder, but you can substitute pure vanilla extract here, anywhere from ½–1 teaspoon.

Ideas: For extra flavor, try adding ½ teaspoon or so ground cinnamon and/or nutmeg, or ½–1 teaspoon grated orange or lemon zest. You can also add other pure extracts like almond or orange extract. Beyond seasonings, try some chopped banana, blueberries, or nondairy chocolate chips. (Berries *with* chocolate chips are even better!)

Nonstick Skillet Note: For pancakes, it's important to use a good-quality nonstick skillet. If yours has a worn surface or isn't nonstick, the pancakes will stick!

5
The Salad Bowl

I have some version of a salad bowl just about every day for lunch. With so many incredible salad dressings, along with grains, beans, greens, vegetables, and nuts and seeds, my salads are anything but routine. Here, you'll find a variety of flavorful dressings to add to your go-to greens, as well as complete salads to enjoy all year round—such as a Picnic Pasta Salad and Mediterranean Abundance Salad. Finally, no salad is complete without some delicious toppers, and you'll find those here, too, including Bread-End Croutons and Ma-mesan, my signature nut-free parm.

Cornucopia Salad

Kale combined with sweet potatoes, pomegranate jewels, pumpkin seeds, and a fresh dressing—this is autumnal abundance! This salad fares well as a side salad for a potluck or the holidays, or you can dig in as a full lunch bowl.

Serves 4–6

Few pinches sea salt

4½–5 cups cubed (about 1 inch) orange sweet potato

5 cups stemmed and chopped kale

½ cup Sunny Curry Dressing (page 66) or Buddha Dressing (page 67), or more to taste

¼ cup raw or toasted pumpkin seeds or toasted walnut/pecan pieces

¼ cup pomegranate seeds *or* 2–3 tablespoons dried cranberries

Preheat the oven to 425°F. Line a baking sheet with parchment paper and sprinkle the salt over the parchment.

Spread out the sweet potato cubes on the prepared baking sheet. Bake for 35–40 minutes, tossing with a spatula a few times, until the sweet potatoes are fully tender and browned in spots.

Put the kale in a large bowl. Add the cooked sweet potatoes while still hot/warm to wilt the kale slightly. Toss well, then add your choice of salad dressing, starting with a little less than ½ cup. Work the dressing through the kale and sweet potatoes; add more dressing to your desired level. Once the dressing is incorporated, sprinkle on the pumpkin seeds and pomegranate seeds.

Ideas: Some other ingredients that will work nicely in this salad include ½ cup thinly sliced red bell pepper, 1 cup roasted or steamed chopped cauliflower, finely sliced or chopped red onion (to taste), ½ cup finely shredded red cabbage, or ½ cup chickpeas or a firmer whole grain like farro or wild rice.

> **Recipe Renewal!** This salad keeps well in the fridge for a couple of days. Try it . . .
> - as a base for a lunch bowl, adding extra veggies or beans.
> - in a wrap for a substantial and very nutritious lunch on the go!

Rainbow Slaw

I thought I didn't like cabbage—not when it was served boiled when I was a kid, or even later when I tried coleslaw dishes. Until . . . one day I decided to give red cabbage a try. The color was so enchanting, it just called to me in the grocery store, and I was hooked! Soon after, I developed this salad with red cabbage, some carrot, and some sweetness from julienned apple. If you want to skip the napa cabbage (even though it's milder in flavor), feel free to substitute with some of the other suggested veggies!

Serves 4 or more as a side

Dressing

3 tablespoons thick plain unsweetened nondairy yogurt (see note)

1 tablespoon tahini or almond butter

1 teaspoon Dijon mustard

¾ teaspoon sea salt

⅛ teaspoon ground allspice

2 tablespoons red wine vinegar, apple cider vinegar, or rice vinegar

1 tablespoon coconut nectar or pure maple syrup

Lemon pepper or freshly ground black pepper to taste (optional)

Slaw

2 cups finely sliced or shredded red cabbage

2 cups finely sliced or shredded napa cabbage

1–2 cups julienned apple (see note)

1 cup shredded or julienned carrot

Whisk together all the dressing ingredients in a large bowl.

Add the slaw ingredients and toss to coat. Taste and add extra seasoning as desired, or finish with a good twist of lemon pepper!

Yogurt Note: Brands of nondairy yogurt can vary quite a lot in flavor and texture. I prefer to use a plain soy- or nut-based yogurt here because coconut yogurt can taste too sweet or pronounced in this dressing. Also, try to find a very thick yogurt for this recipe. If you don't have yogurt on hand, or don't want to use it, instead use another ½–1 tablespoon tahini and a teaspoon or so more vinegar if desired.

Apple Note: Gala apples are a good choice here because they don't brown much. Or, try substituting more of another vegetable—see the suggestions below.

Veggie Options: You can play with some other combinations of veg in this slaw; try swapping other vegetables for the napa cabbage, the carrot, or both! For instance:
- 1 cup julienned red bell pepper
- 1 cup julienned cucumber (remove seeds; cut lengthwise)
- ½–1 cup shredded or finely sliced fennel (it has a stronger flavor, so you might want to opt for a little less)
- 1 cup julienned jicama

Idea: If you like dried fruit in a coleslaw, try adding raisins or cranberries.

Sunny Curry Dressing

This dressing has great flavor that isn't overpowering. It's fabulous with winter salads!

Makes about ½ cup

¼ cup unsweetened applesauce

1 tablespoon tahini *or*
2 tablespoons nondairy yogurt (see note)

½ teaspoon yellow mustard

½ teaspoon curry powder

½ teaspoon sea salt

¼ teaspoon (scant) ground cinnamon

Freshly ground black pepper to taste (optional)

2–3 tablespoons water, plus more as needed

2½ tablespoons apple cider vinegar

1–2 tablespoons pure maple syrup

Starting with 2 tablespoons water and 1 tablespoon maple syrup, combine all the ingredients in a blender (or in a deep cup if using an immersion blender). Puree until smooth. If you'd like to thin it, add additional water as desired, but keep in mind that the dressing will thicken with chilling. Taste and season with extra syrup, salt, and/or pepper to taste. Serve immediately or store in an airtight container in the refrigerator for up to a week.

Tahini Note: The addition of a small amount of tahini adds an extra level of thickness and richness to the dressing. If using the tahini, you may need a touch more water to blend and thin to the desired consistency. If you cannot eat sesame, or want to keep the dressing lower-fat, you can certainly leave it out, or use the yogurt alternative.

Serving Suggestion: Try this dressing with my Cornucopia Salad (page 62).

Buddha Dressing

This will become a go-to dressing for you, especially if you are partial to the nooch (nutritional yeast)! It has a gorgeous golden color and that special umami quality. Get blending!

Makes about ¾ cup

¼ cup nutritional yeast

1½ tablespoons tahini (see note)

1 small clove garlic, halved

½ teaspoon yellow mustard

¼ teaspoon sea salt, or to taste (see note)

¼ cup apple cider vinegar

2–3 tablespoons water

1½ tablespoons pure maple syrup

1 tablespoon tamari

Starting with 2 tablespoons of water, combine all the ingredients in a blender (or in a deep cup if using an immersion blender) and puree until smooth. Taste and add additional seasonings if needed; thin with additional water if desired. Serve immediately or store in an airtight container in the fridge for up to a week.

Tahini Note: If you'd like a thicker, richer dressing, use another ½–1 tablespoon tahini.

Salt Note: Depending on the brand and type of tamari used, you may want to omit the salt or add more to taste.

Serving Suggestion: Try this dressing on my Cornucopia Salad (page 62).

Guac Your World Dressing

Calling all avocado lovers! Use as is for an all-around rich yet punchy dressing. Or, amp up the seasonings (as noted) for an avocado-based "kind" Caesar dressing. Either way, this recipe will guac your world!

Makes about 1½ cups

¾ cup avocado flesh (about 1 medium avocado)

½–1 teaspoon Dijon mustard

¾ teaspoon sea salt

1 very small clove garlic *or* ¼ teaspoon garlic powder (optional)

Freshly ground black pepper to taste

¾ cup water, plus more as needed

3 tablespoons fresh lemon or lime juice

1–2 teaspoons pure maple syrup

½ teaspoon grated lemon zest

Starting with ¾ cup water and the lower amounts of mustard and maple syrup, combine all the ingredients except for the lemon zest in a blender (or in a deep cup if using an immersion blender) and puree until very smooth. Stir in the lemon zest. Taste and adjust the seasonings as you like. To thin, add water 1 tablespoon at a time. Serve immediately or refrigerate in an airtight container until ready to use. This dressing is best to use fresh or within a day, since it will oxidize and the color and flavor will change.

Avo-Caesar Upgrade: Bump up the seasonings for an avocado-based Caesar dressing! To the ingredients listed, add:

- Additional ½–1 teaspoon Dijon
- 1 tablespoon nutritional yeast (optional)
- 1–2 teaspoons vegan Worcestershire sauce
- Additional small clove garlic (or just 1 large clove) or ¼ teaspoon garlic powder

Use with all romaine lettuce or try a blend of kale and romaine (I usually go with half and half, but you can try any proportion). If using kale, dress the kale leaves first, following the directions for the Smoky Kale Caesar Salad (page 82). Just before serving, add more dressing, romaine leaves, and any additional add-ins, such as Bread-End Croutons (page 77) and Ma-mesan (page 86).

Ninja Dressing

This dressing uses fresh turmeric along with fresh ginger and black pepper for an anti-inflammatory power punch—vegan ninja style! The sweet potato mellows out the flavors and makes the dressing creamy and rich. You will want to make this one weekly.

Makes about 1¼ cups

⅔ cup cooked sweet potato flesh, cooled

1 tablespoon tahini

1½ teaspoons peeled and roughly chopped fresh ginger

1 teaspoon sliced or chopped fresh turmeric (see note)

½ teaspoon (generous) sea salt

½ teaspoon ground cumin, or more to taste

⅛–¼ teaspoon ground cinnamon

⅛ teaspoon allspice

Few good pinches freshly ground black pepper

1 tablespoon pure maple syrup or other liquid sweetener

3 tablespoons fresh lime juice

½ cup water, or more as needed

Starting with ½ cup water and ⅛ teaspoon cinnamon, combine all the ingredients in a blender and puree until very smooth. Taste and add more cinnamon or other seasonings if desired. To thin the dressing to your desired consistency, add extra water as needed. Serve immediately or store in an airtight container in the fridge for up to 5 days.

Turmeric Note: Fresh turmeric looks much like fresh ginger root, but with smaller, thinner knobs. While I usually remove the peel from fresh ginger, I don't remove the skin from fresh turmeric since it's so thin. However, you may need to trim the ends where they may not be as fresh.

Cilantro Lover's Dressing

It's said that you either love cilantro or hate it. Well, this dressing is for the cilantro lovers! It's vibrant, tangy, and fresh, and pairs spectacularly with Indian curries and Asian- and Mexican-inspired dishes.

Makes just under 1 cup

½ cup (lightly packed) fresh cilantro leaves

2 tablespoons fresh parsley

2 tablespoons pumpkin seeds

½ teaspoon sea salt

¼ teaspoon ground cumin

Few pinches ground allspice

Freshly ground black pepper to taste (optional)

¼ cup water

¼ cup unsweetened applesauce

3–3½ tablespoons fresh lemon or lime juice

1–1½ tablespoons pure maple syrup

1 teaspoon Dijon mustard

Starting with 3 tablespoons lemon/lime juice and 1 tablespoon maple syrup, combine all the ingredients in a blender (see note) and puree until well combined and somewhat smooth. Taste and adjust with extra lemon/lime juice, maple syrup, salt, and/or pepper if desired. Serve immediately or store in an airtight container in the refrigerator for up to 4 days.

Blending Note: Because this dressing doesn't have a large volume of liquid, you will need to either use a small blender jar or double the ingredients. I use my Blendtec Twister Jar, and that works perfectly.

Italian Vinaigrette

Italian dressing is a favorite for many, yet most store-bought dressings have a lot of preservatives, additives, or oil. You'll be surprised just how good this dressing tastes—and how quick it is to make. It will eclipse that stale store-bought Italian dressing and be in regular rotation for daily salads.

Makes about ⅔ cup

2 teaspoons nutritional yeast

1½ teaspoons dried basil

1 teaspoon sea salt

½ teaspoon dried oregano

½ teaspoon garlic powder

¼ teaspoon celery seed

⅛ teaspoon freshly ground black pepper

Pinch crushed red pepper (see note)

¼ cup red wine vinegar

¼ cup water

2 tablespoons pure maple syrup

1 tablespoon fresh lemon juice

½–1 tablespoon tahini

1 teaspoon Dijon mustard

Combine all the ingredients in a blender and puree until smooth. Taste and add extra salt and/or pepper if desired. Serve immediately or store in an airtight container in the refrigerator for up to a week.

Red Pepper Note: Use just a couple pinches of crushed red pepper—unless you like more heat!

Serving Suggestion: Try this with the Picnic Pasta Salad (page 78).

Creamy House Dressing

This thick, creamy dressing has no added oil, and it packs a great umami punch with the combination of seasonings. It's quick and easy and might just become your new staple sauce!

Makes about 1 cup

½ cup soaked and drained raw cashews (see page 12)

⅛ teaspoon salt

Freshly ground black pepper to taste

1 tablespoon sliced green onion

⅓–½ cup water

1½–2 tablespoons red wine vinegar

1 tablespoon tahini

1 tablespoon tamari or coconut aminos

2 teaspoons pure maple syrup

1 rounded teaspoon Dijon mustard

Starting with 1½ tablespoons vinegar, combine all the ingredients in a blender (or in a deep cup if using an immersion blender) and process until smooth and creamy. If using a high-powered blender, this will smooth out very quickly. If using a standard blender/immersion blender, it will take a few minutes. Taste and add additional vinegar if desired. Store in an airtight container in the refrigerator for up to 5–6 days.

Ranch Dressing: I hear from readers all the time requesting ranch dressing recipes. This recipe easily converts into a ranch dressing. Simply omit the tamari and increase the salt to ½ teaspoon. Add ½ teaspoon dill seed, ½ teaspoon onion powder, and ¼ teaspoon garlic powder. Presto! A ranch dressing that is better than any store-bought.

Mediterranean Abundance Salad

I love this salad. A vibrant dressing worked into hearty beans and rice, with some Mediterranean vegetables and topped with croutons—salad abundance! If you have sumac on hand, you can also add some of this spice for a Fattoush Salad (see note).

Salad serves 4–5; makes about ¾ cup dressing

Dressing

½ teaspoon dried oregano

½ teaspoon dried basil leaves

¼ teaspoon (rounded) ground allspice

¾ teaspoon (rounded) sea salt

½ small clove garlic

1½ tablespoons sunflower seeds *or* 1½ teaspoons ground chia seeds

Freshly ground black pepper to taste

¼–⅓ cup water

¼ cup red wine vinegar

2½ tablespoons pure maple syrup

1½–2 teaspoons Dijon mustard

Salad

1 (16-ounce) can white beans, rinsed and drained

1 (16-ounce) can chickpeas, rinsed and drained

1½ cups cooked brown rice, chilled

1 cup chopped cucumber (seeded if desired)

1 cup chopped bell pepper (any color)

1 cup chopped tomatoes or sliced cherry or grape tomatoes

½ cup sliced pitted kalamata olives

¼ cup chopped fresh chives, sliced green onion, or chopped red onion

1½ teaspoons chopped fresh oregano (see note)

½ cup crumbled vegan feta (optional)

1 batch Bread-End Croutons (page 77; optional)

Starting with ¼ cup water, combine all the dressing ingredients in a blender and puree until very smooth. Taste and add extra salt and/or pepper as needed; thin with additional water as desired. Serve immediately or store in an airtight container in the refrigerator for up to a week.

In a large bowl, combine all the salad ingredients except the optional feta and croutons. Add the dressing, using anywhere from ½ cup to the full batch, to your preference. Top with the feta and croutons (if using).

Oregano Note: If you don't have fresh oregano, simply omit it from the salad and use another ½ teaspoon dried oregano in the dressing.

Dressing Prep: Since this dressing isn't a large volume of liquid, you will need to either use a small blender jar or double the ingredients. I use my Blendtec Twister Jar, and that works perfectly.

Fattoush Salad: Add ½–1 teaspoon ground sumac to the dressing, along with a touch of fresh garlic. Top the salad with the optional croutons.

Bread-End Croutons

What do you do with the end pieces of sliced bread? Make croutons! You need only 2–3 slices of bread for this recipe, but you can always keep extras in a freezer bag for whenever you want to make croutons.

Makes 2–2½ cups (serves 4)

1 clove garlic, peeled

1 tablespoon aquafaba (see note)

¼ teaspoon (scant) sea salt

¼ teaspoon onion powder

¼ teaspoon paprika or smoked paprika

2–2½ cups cubed or torn ends of bread (see note)

Preheat the oven to 375°F. Line a rimmed baking sheet with parchment paper.

Cut the garlic clove in half and rub the cut side of each half generously around the bottom and insides of a large bowl (this will infuse a garlic flavor that isn't too intense). Discard any remaining garlic or save it for another cooking purpose. Add the aquafaba, salt, onion powder, and paprika to the bowl and whisk to combine. Coat the inner surface of the bowl with the whisked mixture, then add the bread pieces and immediately toss to coat them as evenly as possible.

Transfer the seasoned bread to the prepared baking sheet and spread them out in a single layer. Bake for 7–9 minutes, stirring with a spatula once or twice to ensure they brown evenly. Check the croutons after 7 minutes or so; if they look golden and are becoming crisp, remove (they will crisp more as they cool). If not, bake for another minute, checking them frequently, as they can turn from golden to burned quickly! Store in an airtight container at room temperature for up to a few days or in the refrigerator for 1–2 weeks.

Aquafaba Note: See page 24 for more on aquafaba. In this recipe, it helps the seasonings hold and the croutons crisp nicely without the use of oil.

Bread Note: Some bread ends are thinner, and these are awesome for the croutons! You can even try making croutons from pita breads. If you have thicker slices, try to slice some pieces in half to make them thinner. The bread pieces don't have to be exactly measured to 2½ cups—this recipe is flexible!

Picnic Pasta Salad

This is the ultimate crowd-pleasing pasta salad to bring to a picnic, potluck, or BBQ. It's easy to make, and the flavor of the vinaigrette is spot on!

Serves 4–5

12 ounces dried short pasta, cooked, drained, rinsed, and cooled (see note)

1 cup chopped red, yellow, and/or orange bell pepper

1 cup diced cucumber

1 cup halved or quartered cherry or grape tomatoes

1 cup other favorite veg of choice (see ideas)

½ cup sliced pitted kalamata olives

2–3 tablespoons diced red onion or shallot (optional; see note)

2–3 tablespoons chopped sun-dried tomatoes (optional)

1 batch Italian Vinaigrette (page 72)

Salt and freshly ground black pepper to taste

In a large bowl, combine the pasta, bell pepper, cucumber, tomatoes, other veg, olives, onion (if using), and sun-dried tomatoes (if using). Add the vinaigrette. Stir well to fully coat the pasta and vegetables. Taste and season if desired. Serve, or store in an airtight container in the fridge for up to 3 days (the pasta will continue to absorb the dressing; see pasta note).

Pasta Note: You can use just about any shape or variety of pasta here. I like to use penne or rotini, but you can also use macaroni, bow-tie pasta, or even spaghetti that's been broken into small pieces. Also, you can choose a whole-wheat pasta or other variety. Brown rice pasta can become very hard after refrigerating, however. So, if you want to make this salad and chill it, or have leftovers to refrigerate, brown rice isn't the best option. If you prefer a "saucier" salad, you can use less than 12 ounces of pasta. You can also use a lesser amount of pasta and bump up the amount of veggies! Note that as the pasta sits, it will continue to soak up the dressing—so it's best not to use more than 12 ounces or it will dry out. Cook the pasta in advance until it is just fork-tender (following package directions); if overcooked, the pasta may not hold its shape in the salad. Drain and immediately rinse in cold water to stop the cooking process and ensure the pasta isn't starchy and sticky in the salad. Once rinsed, allow to drain fully to remove excess water.

Veggie Ideas: This is a such a flexible recipe. You can use your favorite vegetables, adjusting amounts to your taste or swapping in for what's listed. Some other options to try: chopped raw or grilled zucchini, chopped grilled onions (delicious!), chopped roasted red bell peppers, thickly grated carrot, sliced artichoke hearts, corn, or green peas.

Onion Note: To take the raw edge off of the onion, soak in a bowl of ice-cold water for 5–10 minutes, then drain. Alternatively, you can omit it or swap in ¼ cup chopped green onion or chives for a milder onion flavor.

"Couch Potato" Salad

Finally, a creamy vegan potato salad that has no mayo and no oil, and is also nut-free. It is fabulously tasty, and I offer you plenty of options to sub in different vegetables and seasonings—as well as a swap to a noncreamy dressing if that's your style (see the dressing note)!

Serves 4 or more; makes just over 1 cup dressing

Salad

2½ pounds new potatoes or cubed red or Yukon Gold potatoes (unpeeled; see note)

Couple pinches sea salt

1 cup chopped green beans

½ cup chopped celery

½ cup chopped dill or sweet pickles

½ cup chopped red or green bell pepper

¼ cup chopped or finely sliced red onion, or more to taste (see note)

2–3 tablespoons chopped fresh dill and/or chives

Creamy Dressing

⅓ cup mixed pumpkin seeds and sunflower seeds

1 teaspoon sea salt

¼ teaspoon dill seed or celery seed (or ¼ teaspoon of each if you like)

½ cup plain unsweetened nondairy milk

⅓ cup plain unsweetened nondairy yogurt (see note)

1½–2 tablespoons rice vinegar or apple cider vinegar

1½ teaspoons pure maple syrup

2 teaspoons Dijon mustard

Put the potatoes in a large pot and cover with cold water. Add a couple pinches of salt. Bring to a boil, then reduce the heat to medium-low and simmer for 10–15 minutes, until almost fork-tender. Add the green beans for the last minute of cooking time. Drain the potatoes and green beans, rinse briefly with cold water, and drain again.

Starting with 1½ tablespoons vinegar, combine all the dressing ingredients in a blender. Puree for a minute or so until smooth. Taste and add additional vinegar or other seasonings as desired. Puree again.

Cut the cooked potatoes into bite-size pieces. Put the potatoes, green beans, celery, pickles, bell pepper, and onion in a large bowl. Add about two-thirds of the dressing and mix well. Add more dressing if desired. Add some of the fresh dill and/or chives and stir to incorporate, then taste and adjust the seasoning as desired. Sprinkle the remaining herbs on top of the potato salad. The salad can be served still a little warm, or you can refrigerate until chilled. Any leftover dressing can be stored in an airtight container for up to 5–6 days.

Potato Prep: It's best not to cut the potatoes too small before cooking, as they will get waterlogged. If using new potatoes, boil them whole and then cut any larger potatoes in half when prepping the salad. If using red or Yukon Gold potatoes, just cut in half or thirds before cooking. Also, I sometimes use potatoes I have baked or steamed/parboiled in advance. It makes for quick prep if you can batch-cook ahead of time! Russet potatoes don't work well in this recipe.

Vegetable Swaps: The consensus on potato salad seems to be that it must include celery, onion, and pickles! If those aren't your favorites, feel free to swap in other veg you like. Some ideas to try: chopped apple (my mom's favorite in potato salad!), sliced radishes, sweet corn, olives, grated carrot, green peas, or chopped cucumber.

Onion Tip: To take the raw edge off the onion, soak in a bowl of ice-cold water for 5–10 minutes, then drain. Alternatively, you can swap out the red onion for green onions or more chives for a milder onion flavor.

Yogurt Note: If you don't have a plain unsweetened yogurt on hand, simply use ¼ cup more milk and 2 teaspoons fresh lemon juice or more vinegar.

Dressing Note: Don't care for creamy dressing in potato salad? Instead use my Italian Vinaigrette (page 72). It's a perfect substitute here!

Recipe Renewal! Have leftover potato salad? Add colorful cooked beans such as black beans or red kidney beans, mix, and serve on a bed of shredded romaine. Or layer in a wrap with hummus or another spread, extra pickles, and any extra veg or fixings.

Smoky Kale Caesar Salad

This creamy, nut-free Caesar dressing gets a hint of smokiness from smoked paprika. I love it on a kale-lettuce combo Caesar salad!

Serves 4 or more; makes about 1½ cups dressing

Smoky Caesar Dressing

½ cup mashed, peeled, and cooked red or Yukon Gold potato, cooled

¼ cup raw pumpkin seeds and/or sunflower seeds

1 small-medium clove garlic or ½ teaspoon garlic powder

2 teaspoons nutritional yeast (optional)

¼ teaspoon smoked paprika

¾ teaspoon sea salt

Freshly ground black pepper to taste

1 cup plain unsweetened nondairy milk

3½–4 tablespoons fresh lemon juice

1 teaspoon Dijon mustard

¼ teaspoon vegan Worcestershire sauce (optional)

2–3 tablespoons water, if needed

Kale Caesar Salad

4–5 cups stemmed and julienned kale leaves (see note)

Few pinches coarse ground or regular sea salt

4–5 cups julienned romaine lettuce leaves

1 batch Potato Croutons (page 85) or Bread-End Croutons (page 77)

Few pinches coarse salt

Freshly ground black pepper to taste

Few pinches smoked paprika (optional)

Lemon wedges, for serving

Starting with 3½ tablespoons lemon juice, combine all the dressing ingredients except the water in a blender (or in a deep cup if using an immersion blender) and puree until very smooth. Add water to thin the dressing if desired. Taste and add additional lemon juice and seasoning as desired.

Toss the kale with about ½ cup of the dressing in a large bowl. Add a few pinches of coarse salt and let sit for 15–30 minutes to slightly wilt and soften the leaves.

Add the lettuce leaves and ¼ cup more dressing. Use tongs to work the dressing through the salad. If desired, add additional dressing to taste. Sprinkle with the croutons and season with salt and pepper. Sprinkle with extra smoked paprika (if using). Serve with lemon wedges.

Note: This dressing thickens after chilling. It's easy to thin out again by adding 2–3 teaspoons water. Or, keep it thick and use as a mayo or dip! Leftovers will keep in an airtight container in the refrigerator for up to 6 days.

Kale Note: If you are new to using kale in a Caesar salad, start with less—maybe just 2 cups—and make up the difference by using extra lettuce. My own family warmed up to kale in salads when I added just a little. As you get the taste for using kale in Caesar and other salads, go ahead and bump it up!

Potato Croutons

These croutons are so much fun! They don't get as crunchy as bread croutons, but that's why I like them. They have a little crispness but are tender enough to pierce with a fork.

Makes 2 cups (serves 3–4)

2 cups cubed (½ inch) cooked red or yellow potatoes, cooled (see note)

1 tablespoon aquafaba (see note on page 24)

1½ teaspoons nutritional yeast

½ teaspoon minced fresh rosemary (optional)

¼ teaspoon sea salt

Preheat the oven to 450°F. Line a rimmed baking sheet with parchment paper. If desired, spray a smidgen of oil on the parchment or wipe over with just a touch of oil (depending on the quality of the parchment paper).

Put the potatoes in a bowl. Add the aquafaba and gently toss. Transfer to the prepared baking sheet and spread out in a single layer. Sprinkle on the seasonings. Bake for 20 minutes, tossing just once, at around the 15-minute mark. After 20 minutes, toss again, then turn off the oven and let the potatoes sit in the warm oven for 10 minutes. Remove, then let cool enough to use as a salad topping. These are best enjoyed fresh and slightly warm, but if you do have leftovers, they can be refrigerated and briefly reheated again to serve.

Potato Note: I use potatoes that I have batch-baked. When I bake potatoes, I always bake extra so I have them on hand for other recipes. Store in the fridge, and you can whip up these croutons in a flash!

Serving Suggestions: Enjoy on salads, but also on soups or pizzas, or simply nibble straight-up!

Ma-mesan (Nut-Free Parm)

I used to always make a nut-based parmesan, or purchase them. Then I realized I could use nutrient-rich seeds more creatively in a parm. After I created this one, my youngest said, "Mom, this is sooo good . . . you should call it 'Ma-mesan'!"

Makes close to 2 cups

½ cup pumpkin seeds

½ cup sunflower seeds (or more pumpkin seeds)

¼ cup nutritional yeast

3 tablespoons coconut flour

3½ tablespoons fresh lemon juice

2 teaspoons chickpea or other mild miso

¼ teaspoon (generous) sea salt

Preheat the oven or toaster oven (see note) to 275°F. Line a rimmed baking sheet with parchment paper.

Put the pumpkin seeds and sunflower seeds in a small food processor. Process until the seeds are crumbly (they don't have to be completely fine). Add the nutritional yeast, coconut flour, lemon juice, chickpea miso, and salt. Pulse a few times to combine.

Transfer the mixture to the prepared baking sheet. Bake for 20–25 minutes, keeping an eye on it and stirring a couple of times to distribute the seeds from the outer edges to the inner. This will keep the outer edges from getting too browned. Turn off the oven and let the mixture sit in the warm oven for another 15–20 minutes. Serve warm, or let cool completely and store in an airtight container in the fridge for up to several weeks.

Toaster Oven Note: This is a small batch, so you can easily use a toaster oven to bake. Do keep a close eye on it, as it can very quickly get too browned in a toaster oven.

Seasoned Balsamic Reduction

Balsamic reductions add finishing flavor to so many dishes! You can buy it in most stores, and many seasoned varieties are available. But you can also make your own!

Makes about ⅓ cup

½ cup balsamic vinegar

1 tablespoon date syrup or pure maple syrup

Couple pinches salt

1 sprig fresh rosemary *or* 1 teaspoon grated orange zest *or* ¼ teaspoon pure vanilla bean powder

In a small saucepan, combine the vinegar, syrup, and salt. Bring the mixture to a boil over medium-high heat, then reduce the heat to low and add the rosemary sprig (if using). Let the mixture simmer for about 25 minutes, stirring occasionally. If the vinegar is sticking to the pan, take it off the heat temporarily, whisk to release any sticky bits, then allow it to resume thickening on the lowest heat setting. After 25 minutes, it should be thickened and have reduced in volume. If you'd like it thicker, let it cook for another few minutes. Remove and discard the rosemary sprig. Alternatively, if you'd like to flavor with the orange zest or vanilla, add it now and stir well. Allow to cool; it will thicken more with cooling. Transfer to an airtight jar or a squeeze bottle (see note).

Idea: If you already know you love balsamic reduction, double this batch so you have a larger amount on hand.

Storing Note: I opt to refrigerate my balsamic reduction if I don't plan to use it within a week or so. After refrigerating, this reduction will thicken and become difficult to pour. Allow it to come to room temperature before using. Balsamic reduction will keep for months in the fridge.

Sunflower Salad

The ingredients in this salad are fresh and nutrient-dense, with white beans, corn, and fresh herbs. The sunflower dressing is lightly creamy, tangy-sweet, and a little smoky. Altogether delicious!

Serves 3–4; makes about ½ cup dressing

Dressing

1½ tablespoons raw sunflower seeds or pumpkin seeds

½ teaspoon sea salt

½ teaspoon smoked paprika

¼ teaspoon ground cumin

¼ teaspoon dill seed (optional; don't substitute dried dill weed)

¼ teaspoon chipotle powder (see note)

2½ tablespoons pure maple syrup

2 tablespoons fresh lime juice

2 tablespoons red wine vinegar or apple cider vinegar

1 tablespoon Dijon mustard

Salad

2 (14–15-ounce) cans white beans, rinsed and drained

1 cup fresh, frozen (thawed), or canned (drained) corn kernels

1 cup cubed (½ inch) cooked red or yellow potato

½ cup finely chopped red bell pepper

½ cup julienned spinach leaves

¼ cup chopped fresh cilantro or basil

2 tablespoons finely chopped sun-dried tomatoes (optional)

Combine all the dressing ingredients in a blender. Puree until very smooth.

Combine all the salad ingredients in a large bowl and toss well.

Add the dressing to the salad and gently stir. Taste and add additional seasoning if desired.

Chipotle Note: If you don't have chipotle powder, use additional smoked paprika instead.

Idea: Instead of potatoes, you could sub in a cooked grain like brown rice or quinoa.

Serving Suggestions: Serve alongside grilled vegetables in the summer; in cooler months, pair with a warm grain and greens. Also try in a tortilla wrap with a little chopped avocado.

Recipe Renewal!

- Serve alongside baked purple or orange sweet potatoes. Try "stuffing" the potatoes once slightly cool with the salad—delicious!
- Make a Buddha bowl: Serve the salad over steamed kale and a cooked grain (warm or cold). Drizzle on extra balsamic reduction to serve.
- Fill a whole-grain tortilla with the salad and any other add-ins and roll it up. To help the mixture hold in the wrap, spread a thick layer of hummus or nut cheese on the tortilla.

Summer Chickpea Salad

This salad is a snap to make, and satisfying just as it is—although, of course, I have ideas for you to make it more of a meal!

Serves 2 or more

Dressing

½ teaspoon (generous) salt

½ teaspoon grated lemon zest (optional)

Freshly ground black pepper to taste

2–2½ tablespoons apple cider vinegar or fresh lemon juice

1 tablespoon pure maple syrup

1 teaspoon Dijon mustard

Salad

2 cups cooked or canned (rinsed and drained) chickpeas (see note)

1½ cups lightly packed spinach leaves, roughly chopped

1 cup chopped avocado

½ cup chopped tomato

½ cup chopped bell pepper (any color) or cucumber

½ cup halved or sliced black, green, or kalamata pitted olives

⅓ cup torn or chopped basil leaves

2 tablespoons sliced green onions, green part only

1–2 tablespoons Seasoned Balsamic Reduction (page 87), for serving (optional)

In a large bowl, whisk together all the dressing ingredients until well combined. Add all the salad ingredients except the balsamic reduction. Toss gently so as not to squish the avocado too much. Taste and add more salt, pepper, and/or vinegar as desired. When serving, drizzle on the balsamic reduction, if using.

Chickpea Note: I like the firm texture of chickpeas in this salad. If you'd like to try another bean to replace chickpeas, kidney beans or cannellini beans are great options.

Veggie Swaps: Get creative! Instead of cucumbers or bell peppers, try more tomato. The olives can be replaced with ¼ cup chopped sun-dried tomatoes or ½ cup chopped pickles. If you love arugula, use some of that in place of part of the spinach. Try to use veggies that are similar in texture when substituting.

Lower-fat option: If you'd like to reduce the fat, reduce the avocado to just ½ cup and replace the other ½ cup with cubed cooked potato or sweet potato!

Season it up! Garlic lovers can add a small to medium garlic clove (minced) to the vinaigrette. For heat, add a shake of crushed red pepper flakes or a dash of hot sauce.

Storing Note: Avocado oxidizes quickly, so this salad is best eaten the same day. Or, if making ahead, leave out the avocado, store the salad in a covered container in the fridge for up to a few days, and add the avocado just before serving.

Fresh Fruit Salad

Not all salads are savory! Growing up, we often had fruit salad as a snack or treat. Sometimes it was canned, but when it was made fresh—oh, it was the best! This is a template more than a recipe, so you can customize your version anytime using your favorite seasonal fruits. See ideas in the notes.

Serves 6 or more

2 cups cored, chopped apples (peeled if desired; see note)

2 cups cored, chopped fresh pineapple

3 cups tangerine or mandarin sections or peeled, cubed orange

2 cups sliced grapes

1 cup sliced berries, kiwi, or cubed melon (see fruit swaps)

1 tablespoon freshly squeezed orange juice (or 1½ teaspoons fresh lime/lemon juice if you like some sourness)

¼ teaspoon pure vanilla bean powder (optional; see note)

1 teaspoon grated orange or lemon zest

In a large bowl, combine all the ingredients and stir gently. Taste and add additional zest and/or vanilla bean powder if you like.

Apple Note: Gala apples are a great choice for less oxidation, as are Cameo and Ambrosia apples.

Fruit Swaps: Feel free to use other fruits that you really love. Try to work with seasonal fruits, such as berries, stone fruits, and melons in the summer, and fruits like pears, persimmon, pomegranates, and citrus (grapefruit and many orange varieties) in the winter. Bananas are always a great option as well, but keep in mind that they tend to oxidize and get a little mushy.

Vanilla Bean Powder Note: My readers know my love for vanilla bean powder! Sometimes a sprinkle can add that certain "something" to a simple dish like this!

6
Noshing: Dips, Spreads, Nibblers

It's time for snacks, sides, appetizers, and straight-up fun-time foods! For when you need a little nosh (or even if you want to make it a meal!), here you'll find my 'Kin Queso, Good Day Sunshine Hummus, Truffle-Salted Nut Cheese, and, for something a little sweet, Kettle Corn. These recipes also include essential side sauces like sour cream and a versatile cashew cream.

'Kin Queso

There are many vegan and dairy-free cheese sauce and queso recipes, but most have nuts and/or oil. This one has neither—instead, it has pumpkin seeds, which gave it its name! Plus, it's made straight in the blender. It's rich and flavorful, and will for sure become a keeper. If you want to make this a straightforward cheese sauce without the queso flair, see the notes.

Serves 4–6

1 cup cooked red or Yukon Gold potato flesh, cooled

½ cup mixed chopped raw red bell pepper and carrot

⅓ cup raw pumpkin seeds

2 tablespoons nutritional yeast

1 medium-large clove garlic

½–1 teaspoon mild chili powder (adjust to spice preference)

½–¾ teaspoon sea salt

½ teaspoon cumin seed

1¼ cups plain unsweetened nondairy milk, divided

2½ tablespoons fresh lime juice

2 tablespoons canned coconut milk (see note)

Add-Ins for Heat (optional)

1–2 tablespoons brine from jar of jalapeños *or* 2–3 tablespoons chopped jarred jalapeños (see note)

Few pinches crushed red pepper

Few splashes chipotle hot sauce or other hot sauce

Toppings (optional)

Your favorite salsa or pico de gallo

Sliced fresh jalapeños

Chopped fresh cilantro

Lime wedges

Starting with half the milk and ½ teaspoon salt, combine all the queso ingredients (including the optional add-ins for heat) in a high-speed blender (see note for standard blender). Puree and, as the mixture becomes smooth, add the remaining milk. Puree for a couple of minutes, to heat through (use the "soup" feature on your blender if you have one). Taste and season with the extra salt and additional seasonings if desired. Top with any optional toppings you like and serve,

Coconut Milk Note: Choose thick canned coconut milk; it need not be refrigerated. If you don't have coconut milk on hand, use more plain nondairy milk.

Jalapeño Note: If you're adding jalapeño brine, you can blend it with the other ingredients. Stir in the chopped jalapeños after blending.

Blender Note: If using a standard blender, puree the mixture until very smooth, then transfer to a saucepan. Heat over low/low-medium heat for 5–8 minutes, until the mixture begins to slowly bubble and thicken, stirring frequently as it thickens to prevent scorching.

Good Day Sunshine Hummus

This hummus has a good dose of both lemon and lime juice, perfect for those who really love a strong tang in homemade hummus—my daughter Bridget, for one! No need to bring extra lemon wedges to the table for this one. (Well, maybe not!)

Serves 4–6

2 (14-ounce) cans chickpeas, rinsed and drained

1 (14-ounce) can white beans, rinsed and drained

1 medium clove garlic

¾ teaspoon salt

¾ teaspoon sumac (optional; see note)

Lemon pepper or freshly ground black pepper to taste (optional)

¼ cup tahini

¼ cup fresh lemon juice (see note)

3–4 tablespoons fresh lime juice (see note)

1 teaspoon grated lemon zest (see note)

1 teaspoon grated lime zest (see note)

3–4 tablespoons water or several ice cubes to thin as desired

Combine all the ingredients except the zests and water in a food processor. Puree until smooth. If it's too thick, add water 1 tablespoon at a time or an ice cube. Continue until you have a very smooth puree. (Sometimes you need to puree hummus much longer than you think—keep going and be sparing with your water or ice so it doesn't become too watery.) Add the zests and pulse to mix. Taste and season with additional salt and pepper or other spices as desired.

Sumac Note: Sumac adds another layer of lemony flavor to this hummus. If you don't have sumac, you can also try adding ¼ teaspoon ground cumin or smoked paprika for additional flavor, or simply omit it.

Lemon/Lime Note: Since citrus plays such a big flavor role in this hummus, do not substitute store-bought lemon and lime juices. Freshly squeezed juice is important. Plus, you'll need the zest of those lemons and limes for added flavor. Preferably, opt for organic lemons and limes when collecting zest.

Avo-mame Hummus

Combining edamame and green peas along with ripe avocado, this take on hummus is bright, fresh, and creamy!

Serves 4–6

1½ cups frozen shelled edamame, thawed (see note)

1 cup frozen green peas, thawed (see note)

1 cup cubed ripe avocado

1 medium clove garlic (use more if desired)

1¼–1½ teaspoons sea salt

½ teaspoon ground cumin

Freshly ground black pepper to taste

¼–⅓ cup fresh lemon or lime juice

Few ice cubes for blending

Handful fresh basil or cilantro leaves (optional)

½ teaspoon grated lemon or lime zest

In a high-speed blender (see note), combine the edamame, peas, avocado, garlic, salt (starting with 1¼ teaspoons), cumin, pepper, lemon juice (starting with ¼ cup), and 2–3 ice cubes (as needed to get the puree moving, but not so much that it thins out). Puree until smooth, stopping to scrape down the blender as needed. Taste and season with extra salt or lemon juice if desired. If using fresh herbs, pulse them in now, then pulse in the zest. Serve or refrigerate in an airtight container for up to 2–3 days (see note).

Edamame/Green Pea Note: To thaw, put the edamame and peas in separate bowls and cover with boiling water. Do them separately, since edamame will need to soak longer (or require draining and a second soak), whereas green peas will thaw in just a minute when covered with boiling water. Drain well.

Blender Note: This hummus works best blended in a high-speed blender, because it will better pulverize the skins on the green peas. You can use a food processor for this recipe, though the hummus will not be as smooth and you may notice the flecks of green peas. I use my Blendtec Twister Jar for this recipe, and it works beautifully.

Refrigeration Note: Since this dip has a fair amount of avocado, it will oxidize some, and so the dip is best when eaten freshly made. However, you can keep it for a few days in the refrigerator in an airtight container. I prefer to use a deeper, narrower jar or container, to lessen the oxidizing. After refrigerating, you can scrape off the surface layer of the dip where it has discolored and serve the fresher layer of the dip.

Sassy Sour Cream

Now you can enjoy your sour cream either cashew-based or nut-free!

Cashew Version
Makes about 1 cup

⅓ cup soaked and drained raw cashews (see page 12)

¼ teaspoon (generous) sea salt

½ cup plain unsweetened nondairy yogurt (see note)

2 tablespoons refrigerated canned coconut cream (see note)

2 teaspoons fresh lemon juice

1 teaspoon apple cider vinegar or more lemon juice

Sunflower (Nut-Free) Version
Makes about 1¼ cups

⅓ cup cooked potato flesh, cooled (see note)

¼ cup raw sunflower seeds (soaked or unsoaked; see page 12 and note below)

¼ teaspoon (generous) sea salt

½ cup plain unsweetened nondairy yogurt (see note)

2½ tablespoons refrigerated canned coconut cream (see note)

2 teaspoons fresh lemon juice

1 teaspoon apple cider vinegar or more lemon juice

Combine all the ingredients in a blender (high-speed optimal, regular blender will take longer), scraping down the blender as needed. Transfer to a container and refrigerate for a half hour or more to allow the sour cream to firm up before serving.

Yogurt Note: Nondairy yogurts vary greatly by brand. I prefer a soy yogurt here, as coconut yogurt can have a pronounced taste. While a thicker yogurt works best, the potato helps thicken the nut-free version, and if you're using cashews, you can add another 1–2 tablespoons yogurt for thickness, and adjust the salt and seasoning as needed. Also, the sour cream will thicken with refrigeration.

Coconut Cream Note: Use regular (not light) coconut milk in this recipe. Before using, refrigerate the can overnight or for a few days. The thick cream will rise to the top and be easy to scoop and measure. Use only the thick cream (reserve the thin coconut milk for another use).

Potato Note: I like to use a waxy potato, such as Yukon Gold or red. Alternatively, you can replace the potato with ¼ cup roughly crumbled medium-firm tofu.

What-amole

Sometimes one or two avocados do not go very far (at least not in my house—our girls *love* avocados!). So, I've found creative ways to "extend" our avocados in guacamole. Here, I add both sweet potato and white beans. Not only do they bulk up the guac, but they also give it good body and flavor.

Serves 3–4

1½–1¾ cups chopped ripe avocado (2 medium-large avocados)

½ cup cooked yellow sweet potato flesh, cooled (see note)

½ cup cooked or canned (rinsed and drained) white beans (see note)

¾ teaspoon salt

⅓ cup water, or more as desired

3–3½ tablespoons fresh lemon or lime juice

Freshly ground black pepper to taste

2–3 tablespoons chopped fresh cilantro (optional)

In a food processor (I use a mini processor), combine half of the avocado, the sweet potato, beans, salt, water, and lemon juice (starting with 3 tablespoons). Puree until smooth. Add the remaining avocado and pulse, or mash it into the pureed dip. Add more water 1 tablespoon at a time if a thinner consistency is desired. (You can also fully puree it, but I think it's nice to have a slightly chunkier texture.) Taste and add extra lemon juice if desired, then season to taste with extra salt and/or pepper, if needed. Top with the cilantro and serve.

Sweet Potato Note: Usually I offer the option to interchange yellow and orange sweet potatoes. In this recipe, however, I recommend using only yellow sweet potatoes, as orange spuds will muddy the color of the guacamole quite a bit! If you don't have any sweet potato, you can use a waxy white potato, such as Yukon Gold or red. You will need a little more water if using white potato.

White Bean Note: Instead of white beans, try using either frozen green peas or shelled edamame. Simply soak in boiling water until warmed through (this will take longer for edamame, just a couple of minutes for green peas), and then drain to use.

Flavor Perks: If you love an extra kick in your guacamole, you can add any or all of the following: ground cumin, chopped fresh cilantro, a couple tablespoons chopped onion, 1 clove minced garlic, ¼ cup chopped pitted olives. Another idea is to stir in ½–1 cup of your favorite salsa.

Truffle-Salted Nut Cheese

I have always loved the essence of truffles, and for many years I could find that flavor only in truffle oil. Then a few years ago I discovered truffle zest and truffle salt. Game changers! I use the truffle zest in this recipe, and it's magical! Truffle salt can also be used, but the amount may need to be adjusted.

Makes about 3 cups

2 cups soaked and drained raw cashews (see page 12 and note below)

1 cup soaked and drained almonds (see page 12 and note below)

1 tablespoon nutritional yeast (optional; see note)

1 small clove garlic (see note)

1¼–1½ teaspoons sea salt

1 teaspoon truffle zest (see note)

¼–⅓ cup fresh lemon juice

2–5 tablespoons water

1 tablespoon white (not dark) balsamic vinegar or red wine vinegar

¼ cup fresh basil leaves or 1–2 teaspoons fresh rosemary leaves (optional)

2 vegan probiotic capsules (optional; see note)

In a food processor or blender, blend the cashews, almonds, nutritional yeast (if using), garlic, 1¼ teaspoons salt, truffle zest, lemon juice, 2 tablespoons water, and the vinegar. Puree and scrape down the sides of the bowl as needed to get the mixture started. Puree again, scrape down again—and puree again! Try not to overwater the cheese early on. Rather, puree much longer than you think you need to, and scrape down in between. If the mixture is stubborn, then add another splash of water. When very smooth, taste. Add more salt or truffle zest as desired, as well as fresh herbs, if using. Puree the herbs briefly. If you want to add the probiotic powder for a more cultured taste, see the note below. Serve, refrigerate in portions for up to a week, or freeze in portions for up to several months.

Nut Note: This cheese is really nice with the combination of cashews and almonds, but you can use all cashews or all almonds if you prefer. If you use all almonds, you may need more water for blending. Try to "skin" the almonds after soaking for a fresher, brighter color in the cheese.

Nutritional Yeast: I use just a smidgen of nutritional yeast in this cheese because I don't want its flavor to be really pronounced. It's optional if you really don't like it or don't have it, but do consider it to add a bit of umami flavor dimension in the background!

Garlic Note: As with the nutritional yeast, subtlety is the name of the game here. Use a small clove, or just a third or half of a regular clove. Do not overpower the cheese with raw garlic.

Truffle Zest Note: I use the Sabatino Tartufi brand of truffle zest. They also make truffle salts. All are incredible! With truffle salts, the level of truffle essence will vary by brand. So, if you don't have the pure zest, omit the salt altogether. Add the truffle salt, starting with 1–1¼ teaspoons, and then add more to taste after pureeing. Either way, the truffle flavor is intoxicating!

Probiotic Culturing: If you'd like to yield more of a cultured flavor from this cheese, you can take another step. After blending, and when you know you don't need to adjust seasonings and use the processor again, remove the blade. Open the probiotic capsules and sprinkle in the powder, then use a wooden spoon or spatula to stir it in (metal can affect the probiotic, which is why it's important to remove the blade and use nonmetal utensils). Transfer the cheese to a nut milk bag or cheese-cloth-lined strainer propped over a bowl. Cover and let sit at room temperature for 24–48 hours. After that time, transfer to the fridge for up to a week, or you can freeze some or all of the cheese for later.

> **Recipe Renewal!** Not just for spreading on breads or crackers, this cheese can be used in lots of creative ways! Try it . . .
> - in Phyllo Phenom Rolls (page 176)
> - as a filling for pasta shells or lasagna (or thinned with more water or nondairy milk to use as a pasta sauce)
> - dolloped on homemade pizzas
> - as a filling for stuffed mushrooms
> - slathered on crostini or heated rolls
>
> **Still have leftovers?** Freeze for later use!

Beany Blinis

I make these unbelievably easy blinis for lunches whenever I need something quick for the fam. We all enjoy having some plain to nibble straight from the pan, and then pairing them up with various toppings and fixings—see the serving ideas. (In fact, you may want to double the batch for a hungry family!)

Makes 16–18 blinis

1 cup chickpea flour

2–3 teaspoons dried onion flakes

¼ teaspoon (generous) sea salt

Freshly ground black pepper to taste

1 cup water

In a mixing bowl, whisk together all the ingredients for a minute or so to fully incorporate the chickpea flour.

Preheat a nonstick skillet over medium-high heat. Ladle a full tablespoon of batter (you can roughly measure or eyeball) into the skillet. Cook for 2–3 minutes, until the batter has formed some bubbles and is beginning to look dry in spots on top. Use a spatula to flip (if they are sticking, they aren't ready). Let cook for another minute or so on the second side. Work in batches, and transfer the cooked blinis to a cooling rack or to a warm (low heat) oven or toaster oven to hold until ready to serve. The blinis will cook a little more quickly as you progress through the batter since the skillet has more even heat; turn the heat down to medium if the blinis are getting too brown before cooking fully in the center.

Optional Spices: We love these fairly plain, just seasoned with the onion flakes and salt. That way we can serve with other pairings we like, kind of like a blini buffet! If you want to add additional flavors, you can try ¼–½ teaspoon ground cumin, smoked paprika, garlic powder, or chili powder. Or, add a couple tablespoons minced fresh dill, oregano, thyme, or cilantro. I recommend fresh herbs over dried since these cook so quickly.

Serving Suggestions: Use blinis to make a sandwich with hummus, sliced veg, and sliced avocado. Or, use in tortilla wraps with dips and veggies. I love them with leftover soups or in a salad bowl, and also with salsa or a creamy salad dressing. So many options with these!

Love 'em? Then you'll probably also love my Zucchini Fritters (page 147)!

Lemon-Herbed Chickpeas

These chickpeas are delicious to nibble on, or to top salads, pasta, soups, pizza, grains, and more! Leftovers can be lightly mashed or pureed with condiments for a sandwich spread.

Serves 4–6

2 (14-ounce) cans chickpeas, rinsed and drained

1 tablespoon minced fresh oregano (reserve a few pinches)

1 tablespoon minced fresh thyme (reserve a few pinches)

1 tablespoon minced fresh chives (reserve a few pinches)

½ teaspoon sea salt (rounded)

Lemon pepper or freshly ground black pepper to taste

¼ cup fresh lemon juice

1–1½ tablespoons pure maple syrup

½ teaspoon Dijon mustard (optional)

½ teaspoon grated lemon zest (optional)

Preheat the oven to 450°F. Combine all the ingredients except the optional lemon zest in a baking dish (starting with 1 tablespoon maple syrup, and reserving some of the fresh herbs) and toss to combine. Bake for 25–30 minutes, stirring once or twice, until the chickpeas are a little golden and the marinade is absorbed. Add the reserved fresh herbs and lemon zest (if using) and toss. Taste and add extra seasoning and/or maple syrup if desired. Serve warm!

Kettle Corn

The sweet 'n' salty favorite made at home, without oil or margarine!

Makes about 10 cups, serves 4 as a snack

3 tablespoons unrefined sugar (see note)

2 tablespoons softened coconut butter

1 tablespoon refrigerated canned coconut cream (see note)

¼ teaspoon sea salt

⅓–½ cup organic popcorn kernels (see note)

Preheat the oven to 300°F. Line a rimmed baking sheet with parchment paper.

In a small ovenproof bowl, combine the sugar, coconut butter, coconut cream, and salt. Put the bowl in the oven for 5 minutes or so to soften (alternatively, you can place the bowl in a hot water bath). You want it warm enough that you can easily stir the ingredients together.

Pour the mixture into a very large bowl (one that you will use to collect the popcorn) and smooth the mixture around the bottom and sides of the bowl. Pop the popcorn (see note), collecting it in that large bowl if using an air popper. As the popcorn begins to fill the bowl, use your hands or a spatula to move it around and gently coat it with the mixture. Try not to break up the popcorn too much, just gently move it around so the heat of the popcorn will help melt and distribute the coating.

Transfer the coated popcorn to the prepared baking sheet. Spread it fairly evenly over the pan, and if there is any coating left in your mixing bowl, use a spatula to scrape it out and work it among the popcorn. Bake for 8–9 minutes, then immediately turn off the oven and let the popcorn sit in the warm oven for another 7–8 minutes. Taste and add a touch more salt if desired. Let cool further on the countertop, then enjoy!

Sugar Note: Coconut or date sugar can be substituted. They will result in a darker color.

Coconut Cream Note: Use regular coconut milk (rather than light) in this recipe. Before using, refrigerate the can overnight or for a few days. The thick cream will rise to the top and be easy to scoop and measure. Use only the thick cream (reserve the thin coconut milk for another use).

Popcorn Note: An air popper works best for popping corn without any oil or butter. If you think you'll like more coating on the popcorn (as I do!), use closer to ⅓ cup of kernels. For greater yield, and less coating, use the full ½ cup of kernels. If you don't have an air popper, you can still pop the corn on the stovetop, but the kernels won't pop as fully. Heat a large pot over medium-high heat. Add the kernels to the pot and put on the lid. As the pot heats, begin shaking it at frequent intervals. Within the first minute, the popcorn should begin to pop. Continue shaking the pot often until the popping slows down, then remove the pot from the heat and release the lid just slightly to let some steam escape. Once the popping has fully stopped, remove the lid and transfer the popcorn to the bowl with the sugar mixture and proceed with the recipe.

Cashew Cream

This sauce is creamy and luscious with a cooling quality that makes it great to pair with spicy dishes. Try it in the No Butter No Chicken (page 191) or whenever you want a cream-like topping.

Makes about 1⅓ cups

1 cup soaked and drained raw cashews (see page 12)

¼ teaspoon (generous) sea salt

½ cup water, plus more as needed (see note)

1 tablespoon fresh lemon juice

Combine all the ingredients in a blender (or in a deep cup if using an immersion blender. Puree until very smooth, scraping down the blender as needed. If not fully smooth, puree again and add another few teaspoons water if needed (see note). Serve or store in an airtight container in the refrigerator for up to 6 days. If you don't plan to use it within this time, transfer to the freezer.

Water Note: Usually ½ cup water is enough to yield a thick, velvety cream. However, if your cashews aren't as swelled, or if you don't have a high-speed blender, you may find it helpful to add another splash of water. Also, the consistency of this cream is quite thick, ideal as a topping to dollop on baked potatoes or even as a dip (see ideas). Feel free to thin the cream with extra water to use it more like a sauce—for instance, to drizzle on pizza, enchiladas, burritos, or curry dishes.

Ideas: Remember onion dip for chips? I do! Keep this cream thick and stir in 1–2 tablespoons dried onion flakes. Let sit until the onion absorbs the moisture. Other ideas for seasonings include a sprinkle of smoked paprika or curry powder, or try mixing minced fresh dill or basil into the cream.

Potato Flatbreads

Who knew potatoes could be so versatile? Minimally seasoned, these easy-to-make flatbreads go with many dishes and won't overpower the flavor. (Of course, you can add more seasonings if you like!)

Makes about 8 small flatbreads

2 cups cooked red or Yukon Gold potato flesh, cooled

1 cup almond meal (see note for nut-free)

½ cup oat flour

½ teaspoon baking soda

½ teaspoon sea salt

1½ teaspoons red wine vinegar

Combine all the ingredients in a food processor. Pulse to begin to incorporate the ingredients, then process until the mixture begins to get sticky and form a dough-like consistency on the blade. This won't take long, about a minute or two.

Preheat a nonstick skillet over medium-high heat. Take a small scoop of dough (about ⅓ cup) and roll it a little in your hands. Place it between two sheets of parchment paper. Use a rolling pin to lightly roll out the dough, moving from the inside out and turning the dough as you go. It can be uneven and rustic; it doesn't have to form a perfect circle. Once you have a shape 5½–6½ inches across, remove it from the parchment and place it in the heated skillet. Cook for 2–3 minutes on the first side, until golden. Flip and cook for another 2 minutes, or until golden on the other side. Transfer to a cooling rack just a little while. Serve warm or cooled. Store leftovers in an airtight container in the refrigerator for up to a week (see recipe renewal note).

Nut-Free Note: The nut-free version of these flatbreads is great—I urge you to try it even if you don't have a nut allergy! Use 1 generous cup raw pumpkin seeds in place of the almond meal. (Roasted pumpkin seeds can be used, but they usually have salt, so check the label. If they have salt, you may want to omit the salt altogether in the recipe.) First, puree the pumpkin seeds on their own in the processor until they reach a fine consistency, much like that of almond flour. Then, add the remaining ingredients and proceed with the recipe.

Recipe Renewal! If you like, you can reheat leftovers in a low oven or toaster oven for a couple of minutes. They get a little crisp and taste a bit like potato chips!

7
Dinner Plates

We've arrived at the main event. Hearty stuff like casseroles, pasta dishes, burgers, and one-pot wonders. I also include soups and stews here. We have always eaten them as dinner, and filled with beans and starchy vegetables, they are so substantial.

Get ready to dig into the most luscious Ulti-Mac, a nut-free Awakened Pad Thai, Lentil and Sweet Potato Meatloaf, Chickpea Satay Casserole, Beyond Beet Burgers, and so much more!

Pressure Cooker Quicken Noodle Soup

This soup looks surprisingly similar to traditional chicken noodle, and because it's made in a pressure cooker, you'll have a comforting bowl of soup ready in very little time. The seasonings give it a fresher and brighter flavor than conventional chicken noodle soup—not to mention more health-promoting properties!

Serves 5–6

2–3 tablespoons water

1½ cups diced onion

1½ cups diced carrot

1–1½ cups diced celery

1 teaspoon garlic powder

½–¾ teaspoon sea salt

½ teaspoon dried thyme

½ teaspoon dried oregano

¼ teaspoon ground sage or dried rosemary

¼ teaspoon ground turmeric (optional)

Freshly ground black pepper to taste

⅓–½ pound dry spaghetti noodles of choice, broken into thirds (see note)

1½ cups crumbled firm or extra-firm tofu (see note)

2 bay leaves

5–5½ cups boiling water

2 cups vegetable broth

¼ cup minced fresh parsley, plus more for optional garnish

Set a multifunction pressure cooker (such as an Instant Pot) to sauté. Pour in the 2–3 tablespoons water and add the onion, carrot, celery, garlic powder, ½ teaspoon salt, thyme, oregano, sage, turmeric (if using), and pepper to taste. Cook, stirring, for 4–5 minutes. Add the spaghetti, tofu, bay leaves, boiling water (5 cups for lesser amount of pasta, 5½ cups for more pasta), and broth. Gently stir.

Secure the lid and set the valve to the "sealed" position. Press the Manual button, then set the cook time for 3 minutes at high pressure. Allow the pot to come to pressure and cook. Once the timer goes off, turn off the pot and allow the pressure to naturally release for 15 minutes. After 15 minutes, release the lid and stir in the parsley and let sit for a couple of minutes. Taste and season with extra salt and/or pepper if desired, and sprinkle with the optional parsley garnish.

Water Note: When it comes time to add the water and broth, using boiling water helps bring the cooker to pressure faster.

Spaghetti Note: You can use any spaghetti noodle you like—whole-wheat, brown rice, or another variety—or even cut pasta like rotini or penne. Brown rice pasta, which is starchy, will make the broth thicker. But brown rice noodles can also stick together easily, so be sure to stir them into the liquid when you first add them. Cooking times vary based on the type of pasta, so having a short cooking time and natural release helps avoid overcooking.

Tofu Note: If you first freeze the tofu, then thaw it, it will be drier and crumblier, which works well in this soup. To hasten thawing, you can place the frozen, unopened package of tofu in a bowl of very hot water and replace the hot water several times within a half hour. Continue until the tofu has thawed through, or mostly thawed. Be sure to squeeze out excess water once it's thawed. You won't use the entire package for this soup, so you can save the remainder for another use.

Aush Soup

Aush is a traditional Afghan noodle soup. I first tried it at a local Afghan restaurant and loved it! The complexity of flavors from the combination of spices and herbs is enchanting. However, many aush recipes call for a lot of oil. This version brings forth the body and flavors without the use of oil.

Serves 4–5

2 tablespoons plus 6 cups water, divided, plus more as needed (see note)

2 cups chopped onion

½ cup diced carrot

½ cup diced celery

1 tablespoon ground coriander

1 tablespoon ground paprika

1½–2 teaspoons ground turmeric

1 teaspoon sumac (optional; see note)

1 teaspoon salt

¼ teaspoon ground cinnamon (optional)

3 large cloves garlic, minced

1–2 (15-ounce) cans chickpeas and/or kidney beans

2 cups vegetable broth

¼ cup tomato paste

½ pound spaghetti noodles of choice, broken into thirds

3–4 cups chopped spinach or kale

½ cup chopped fresh cilantro

¼ cup chopped fresh mint

½–1 teaspoon grated lemon zest

2–3 tablespoons fresh lemon juice

Pour 2 tablespoons water into a large soup pot and set over medium-high heat. Add the onion, carrot, celery, coriander, paprika, turmeric (starting with 1½ teaspoons), sumac (if using), salt, and cinnamon (if using). Cook for 4–5 minutes to begin to soften the vegetables, adding another splash of water if the mixture is sticking. Add the garlic, stir, and cook for another 1–2 minutes, until fragrant.

Add the chickpeas, 6 cups water, vegetable broth, and tomato paste and stir. Increase the heat to high to bring the soup to a boil, then reduce the heat to low, cover, and simmer for 10 minutes. Remove the lid, increase the heat to bring back to a boil, and add the broken spaghetti noodles. Let the mixture come back to a boil, and reduce the heat slightly if boiling too vigorously. Cook until the spaghetti is tender (this will vary based on the noodle variety, but usually 7–8 minutes). If the soup seems too thick, add additional water.

Add the spinach, cilantro, mint, lemon zest, and lemon juice (starting with 2 tablespoons). Add a touch more water if desired, and add more turmeric and/or lemon zest and juice if desired.

Water Note: This soup will thicken as the pasta cooks. It also thickens considerably as the soup sits on the stovetop after making it; leftovers will continue to thicken up in the fridge. The 6-plus cups of water in this soup, along with the 2 cups of vegetable broth, should give a nice volume of liquid when first cooking. Of course, you can always thin it out with more water after the soup sits and when you reheat any leftovers.

Sumac Note: Sumac adds a bright, lemony, slightly floral note to this soup. It's not an especially common spice, so you may not see it in your grocery store. It might be found in the international foods section with other spices. Or, you may need to shop at a specialty or natural foods store or online.

Curried Carrot and Lentil Soup

The ingredients in this soup are simple, but the flavors are full, with warm curry and creamy coconut. If you prefer a chunkier soup, you can skip the pureeing step, or puree just partially to leave some texture.

Serves 4 or more

2–3 tablespoons plus 4 cups water, divided

4 cups sliced carrots

1 cup chopped onion

1 cup chopped celery

1½ tablespoons curry powder

1–1¼ teaspoons sea salt

¼ teaspoon ground allspice, plus a pinch for optional garnish

⅛ teaspoon chipotle powder, plus a pinch for optional garnish (see note)

1 cup red lentils, rinsed and drained

1 cup canned coconut milk

3–4 tablespoons fresh lemon or lime juice

4–5 tablespoons chopped fresh cilantro, for serving (optional)

Pour 2 tablespoons water into a large soup pot and set over medium-high heat. Add the carrots, onion, celery, curry powder, salt (starting with 1 teaspoon), allspice, and chipotle powder. Cook for 7–8 minutes, until the onion and carrot have softened, adding more water if the veggies are sticking.

Add the lentils, 4 cups water, and coconut milk and stir. Increase the heat to high to bring the soup to a boil, then reduce the heat to low, cover, and simmer for 15–20 minutes, stirring once halfway though, until the lentils are fully softened.

Add 3 tablespoons lemon or lime juice. Use an immersion blender to puree the soup to your desired consistency. Alternatively, you can transfer the soup in batches to a blender and puree. Taste and add extra salt and lemon juice if needed. Divide the soup into bowls and serve sprinkled with cilantro and a pinch of allspice and/or chipotle powder, if desired.

Chipotle Note: There's just a small amount of chipotle powder here, so as not to overpower the other flavors. A pinch or two gives a certain "something" in the background, especially if your curry powder is mild. If you don't want any chipotle powder, feel free to omit. If you want to increase it, do so very modestly. Try another ⅛ teaspoon to start, and then determine if you want more.

Greens Boost: Before serving, add several cups of baby spinach and stir until just wilted.

Recipe Renewal! You can keep extra soup in the fridge for several days; the flavors will only improve! This soup also freezes well if you want to double the batch. To revamp leftovers as a new meal, gently reheat and try it . . .

- as a "sauce" over cooked rice and baked sweet potatoes.
- tossed into hot pasta.
- mixed into beans and greens for a lunch bowl, topped with other vegetables, a sprinkle of pumpkin seeds, and some cubed avocado.

Aromatic Thai Noodle Stew

One of my darling recipe testers said, "This is such a smart recipe, no added oil, little salt but big on flavor!" Big on flavor it is—but not big on fuss.

Serves 3–4

1 (13½-ounce) can coconut milk, divided

1 cup peeled and chopped sweet potato or butternut squash (see note)

1 cup chopped carrot (see note)

1½ tablespoons peeled and chopped fresh ginger

3 cloves garlic, quartered

1 teaspoon salt

3½–4 cups water, divided

3½–4 tablespoons Thai red or yellow curry paste

½ (16-ounce) package rice sticks/noodles

2 cups cooked or canned (rinsed and drained) black beans (see note)

½ cup frozen corn kernels

½ cup diced red bell pepper

2½–3½ tablespoons fresh lime juice

5–6 cups spinach leaves (see note)

½ cup chopped fresh cilantro, plus more for optional garnish

2 tablespoons chopped green onion, plus more for optional garnish

½ teaspoon grated lime zest

Lime wedges (optional)

Hot sauce (optional)

Pour about ¼ cup of the coconut milk into a large soup pot and set over medium-high heat. Add the sweet potato, carrot, ginger, garlic, and salt and stir. Add 2 cups of the water. Increase the heat to high to bring the soup to a boil, then reduce the heat to low, cover, and simmer for 8–10 minutes, until the veggies have softened. Remove from the heat and use an immersion blender to puree this soup base. If you don't have an immersion blender, allow the mixture to cool slightly, transfer to a blender to puree, then return to the pot.

Add the Thai curry paste (starting with 3½ tablespoons), remaining coconut milk, and another 1½ cups water and stir. Break the rice noodles into halves or thirds and add to the soup, along with the beans, corn, bell pepper, and lime juice (starting with 2½ tablespoons) and stir. Increase the heat to high to bring to a boil, then reduce the heat to low, cover, and simmer for another 2–4 minutes, just long enough to soften the noodles. Remove from the heat. Finish the soup by adding the spinach, cilantro, green onion, and lime zest. Taste and add more Thai curry paste, lime juice, or salt to taste. Serve sprinkled with extra cilantro and green onion, and serve with lime wedges and hot sauce, if desired.

Sweet Potato/Squash/Carrot Note: Frozen butternut squash and carrot work well in this recipe, and they don't even need to be thawed first—just throw them in the pot. If you don't have carrots, feel free to substitute more sweet potato or squash.

Black Bean Note: If using canned beans, 2 cups of black beans is a little more than one 14- or 15-ounce can. You can simply use 1 can, rinsed and drained, or measure out more black beans from 2 cans—or feel free to use the full 2 cans!

Spinach Note: Instead of spinach, or to replace some of it, you can use finely sliced or shredded savoy or red cabbage. If using red cabbage, the color can leach into the stew if cooked too long, so add it just before serving.

Idea: An alternative to black beans (or to use in addition to black beans) is to dry-bake tofu for a topping. Crumble firm tofu into small chunks and scatter them on a rimmed baking sheet lined with parchment paper. Sprinkle with 1 tablespoon tamari. Bake at 400°F for 20–25 minutes. Allow to cool, then crumble over finished portions of this stew.

White Bean and Corn Chowder

Tasty, comforting, satisfying! This soup has it all—including the option to add those greens!

Serves 4–6

3–4 tablespoons dry white wine or water

2 cups chopped onion

1 cup chopped celery

2 cloves garlic, minced, or 2 teaspoons garlic powder

2 teaspoons dried basil

2 teaspoons dried oregano

1½ teaspoons dried thyme

1½ teaspoons dry mustard

½ teaspoon salt, or more to taste

Freshly ground black pepper to taste

2–3 cups cubed red or Yukon Gold potatoes (see note)

1–1½ cups diced red bell pepper

2 (15-ounce) cans white beans, rinsed and drained (reserve about ½ cup for blending)

2 bay leaves

2 cups vegetable broth

2 cups water

½ cup plus ¾ cup corn kernels (thawed if frozen), divided

1 cup plain unsweetened nondairy milk

2–3 cups chopped kale or spinach leaves (optional)

Few dashes chipotle hot sauce or other hot sauce (optional)

2–3 tablespoons chopped fresh chives, for serving (optional)

Pour 3 tablespoons wine or water into a large soup pot and set over medium-high heat. Add the onion, celery, garlic, spices, salt, and pepper. Cook, stirring, for 4–5 minutes, until the onion is slightly soft, adding another splash of wine or water if the mixture is sticking.

Add the potatoes, bell pepper, white beans (except reserved ½ cup), bay leaves, broth, and 2 cups water. Increase the heat to high to bring the mixture to a boil. Reduce the heat to low, cover, and simmer for 10–15 minutes, until the potatoes are fork-tender.

Meanwhile, combine the reserved ½ cup beans, ½ cup corn, and milk in a blender (or in a deep cup if using an immersion blender). Puree until fully smooth. Add the puree to the soup while the potatoes are still cooking.

Once the potatoes are cooked through, add the remaining ¾ cup corn kernels and stir. The corn only needs to heat for a couple of minutes. If adding the greens, stir these in as well (spinach will wilt almost immediately with the heat of the soup; kale will take a few minutes to wilt). Once ready, taste and season with additional salt and pepper, if you like, or with a couple of dashes of hot sauce. Serve, sprinkled with the fresh chives, if desired.

Potato Note: If you'd like to use a grain instead of potato, use ⅓ cup dry quinoa and add another ½–1 cup water.

A-Game Chili

I have made many a chili recipe, and this one is a hot favorite! Don't be leery of the buckwheat groats; I am not usually a huge buckwheat fan, but they *work* in this recipe, giving a wonderfully chewy and substantial texture. Depending on how much heat you enjoy in your chili, you can kick up the spices or tone them down as needed.

Serves 5 or more

3 tablespoons dry red wine (see note)

9–10 cups chopped portobello or cremini mushrooms (just under 2 pounds; see note)

1½–2 cups diced onion

4–5 teaspoons mild chili powder

2–3 teaspoons smoked paprika

1½ teaspoons dried oregano

½ teaspoon ground cumin

¼ teaspoon ground allspice

½ teaspoon crushed red pepper, or to taste

1 teaspoon sea salt, or to taste

2 cups diced bell pepper

1 cup diced zucchini

½ cup buckwheat groats

½ cup tomato paste

3 large cloves garlic, minced

1 (14-ounce) can pinto beans, rinsed and drained

1 (14-ounce) can black beans, rinsed and drained

1 (14-ounce) can kidney beans or additional black beans, rinsed and drained

2 tablespoons chopped sun-dried tomatoes

3 cups water

1 teaspoon molasses

½–1 cup frozen corn kernels

Hot sauce, for serving (optional)

Lime wedges, for serving

Pour the wine into a large soup pot and set over medium-high heat. Add the mushrooms, onion, spices, and salt. Cook for 10 minutes, stirring occasionally, to allow the mushrooms to release their moisture and the onion to soften. (The mushrooms will release enough moisture to prevent sticking.)

Add the bell pepper, zucchini, buckwheat, tomato paste, and garlic and cook, stirring often, for 3–4 minutes. Add the beans, sun-dried tomatoes, water, and molasses and stir. Increase the heat to high to bring the chili to a boil, then reduce the heat to low, cover, and simmer for 20–25 minutes, until the buckwheat is fully cooked.

Stir in the corn and allow to heat through for a couple of minutes. Taste and adjust the seasoning as desired. Serve with hot sauce, if desired, and lime wedges.

Wine Note: Instead of wine, you can use 2 tablespoons balsamic vinegar plus 1 tablespoon water or juice.

Mushroom Note: The mushrooms add great texture to this chili, along with the beans and buckwheat. If, however, you are not a mushroom lover, here are some suggestions for substitutions for the mushrooms (keep in mind that they reduce quite a lot with cooking):

- 1–2 cups finely chopped cauliflower (or 2 cups store-bought cauliflower rice) and another 1–2 cups diced zucchini
- Another ½ cup buckwheat groats and another 1 cup diced zucchini (you may need to add more water)
- 1 (7- or 8-ounce) package tempeh, finely chopped, and another 1 cup diced bell pepper

Recipe Renewal! To use any leftover chili:

- Spoon onto halved cooked white or sweet potatoes, and bake 'em! Top with vegan cheese before baking, or top with What-amole (page 104) or chopped avocado for serving.
- Make quick tacos using the chili as the filling and adding some chopped lettuce, tomatoes, and avocado as supporting stars! Want something extra? Drizzle the tacos with 'Kin Queso (page 96).
- Make chili dogs (vegan dogs, of course), burritos, quesadillas, or a Mexican lasagna!

Alphabet Soup

This soup was created in homage to Amy's alphabet soup—which all of my children have loved over the years! While decidedly kid-friendly, that doesn't mean this soup can't be enjoyed by adults!

Serves 4–5

2 tablespoons plus 5 cups water, or more as needed, divided

1 cup diced onion

1 cup diced carrot

1 teaspoon dried basil

¼ teaspoon garlic powder

1–1¼ teaspoons sea salt

2 cups diced red or yellow potatoes (not russet)

½ cup tomato paste

1 cup cooked or canned (rinsed and drained) beans of choice (see note)

1 cup alphabet pasta (see note)

1½ tablespoons pure maple syrup (optional; see note)

1 cup fresh or frozen green peas

1 cup fresh or frozen corn kernels

Pour 2 tablespoons water into a large pot and set over medium-high heat. Add the onion, carrot, basil, garlic powder, and salt (start with 1 teaspoon). Cover and cook for 5–7 minutes, stirring once or twice, until the onion and carrot start to soften. Add the potatoes, tomato paste, beans, and 5 cups water. Increase the heat to high to bring to a boil, then reduce the heat to medium-low, cover, and simmer for about 10 minutes, until the potatoes are nearly fork-tender. Stir in the pasta and cook for 4–8 minutes longer, until both the pasta and potatoes are cooked through (try not to overcook the pasta, as it will become mushy). Add the maple syrup, if desired. Stir in the peas and corn and let sit for 2–3 minutes to heat through. Thin with more water if needed and season to taste with extra salt if desired. Divide the soup between bowls and serve.

Bean Note: If you're using canned beans, go ahead and use the full can rather than 1 cup if you prefer. Drain and rinse the beans before putting them in the soup.

Pasta Note: You can use any small pasta shape you like here. If you're having trouble finding alphabet pasta, or need to use a gluten-free pasta, go for another small (and fun!) pasta shape. Note that smaller pasta shapes will cook faster, so check the directions on the box and adjust your cook time accordingly.

Maple Syrup Note: A touch of maple syrup adds that quality of sweetness found in store-bought alphabet soup. If you don't think you want it in there, taste without and then add a small amount to taste when finishing.

Pantry Soup

I sometimes call this a "kitchen sink soup"—using all the common veg you have in the fridge and in your pantry, along with other pantry staples. It's entirely flexible! See the notes for some substitution ideas. Whatever you use, it will turn out delicious and comforting.

Serves 5–6

3–4 tablespoons dry white wine or water

2 cups chopped onion

2 teaspoons Dijon mustard

2 teaspoons dried oregano

1 teaspoon dried rosemary

1 teaspoon dried basil

½ teaspoon dried thyme

½ teaspoon dill seed

½ teaspoon salt

Freshly ground black pepper to taste

4 cups mixed sliced or chopped carrot and celery

4 cloves garlic, minced or grated

6 cups mixed cubed root vegetables and winter squash (see note)

2–3 (14-ounce) cans beans of choice, rinsed and drained (see note)

5 cups water

2 cups vegetable broth

2 dried bay leaves

4–5 cups torn kale or spinach leaves (optional; see note)

1 tablespoon miso (optional)

1 tablespoon apple cider vinegar

Pour the wine into a large soup pot and set over medium-high heat. Add the onion, mustard, oregano, rosemary, basil, thyme, dill seed, salt, and pepper and stir. Cook for 3–4 minutes, stirring frequently. If the vegetables are sticking, add another splash of wine.

Add the carrot, celery, and garlic and stir. Reduce the heat slightly so the garlic doesn't burn, and cook for another couple of minutes. Add the root vegetables and winter squash, beans, broth, and water. Increase the heat to high to bring the soup to a boil, then reduce the heat to low, cover, and simmer for 10–15 minutes, until the root vegetables are tender (this will depend on how large the vegetables are cut and also the type of vegetables used). Remove the soup from the heat. Stir in the greens, miso (if using), and apple cider vinegar and let sit until the greens are just wilted. Taste and season with more salt and/or pepper, if desired. Serve immediately to maintain the vibrant color of the greens.

Root Veggie/Squash Note: I like to use a combo of cubed root vegetables (such as potatoes, sweet potatoes, parsnips, rutabaga, and turnip) and winter squash (acorn, butternut, kabocha, and delicata).

Bean Note: This stew can easily hold 3 cans of beans! I like to use a combination of whatever I have on hand—usually kidney beans, chickpeas, white beans, pinto beans, or black beans. If you're using cooked dried beans instead, two cans is the equivalent of about 3½ cups, and three cans is roughly 4½–5 cups cooked beans.

Kale/Spinach Note: If you have greens like spinach, chard, or kale on hand, it's best to add them just before serving, so they stay bright green and taste the best. Spinach will wilt more quickly than kale.

Veggie Swaps: Can you use other vegetables in this stew? Absolutely! Consider the "hardiness" of the vegetable, and add it to the soup accordingly. For instance, cauliflower will cook a little faster than root vegetables, but it also won't turn "off" in taste or color, so it can be added at the same time. Broccoli, however, will turn in color. So, it's best to add that in the last minute or two of cooking.

Beyond Beet Burgers

Think beyond meat. Beyond store-bought! These burgers are absolutely delicious, made with whole-foods ingredients, and can be prepped in about 10 minutes with a food processor. Yep, these are game changers.

Makes 11–12 patties

1½ cups cubed or sliced raw beet (peeled)

1 cup sliced carrot

1 medium-large clove garlic, peeled (see note)

2 (14-ounce) cans black beans, rinsed and drained

⅓ cup sun-dried tomatoes (not packed in oil; see note)

1 tablespoon fresh rosemary leaves *or* 1 teaspoon dried

1 teaspoon sea salt

½ teaspoon dill seed (see note)

1½ teaspoons balsamic vinegar

1 tablespoon tamari

2½ cups cooked brown rice or jasmine rice, cooled

1½ cups toasted pecans, divided (see note for nut-free)

¾ cup rolled oats

In a large food processor (see note), combine the beet, carrot, and garlic. Process until finely broken down. Add the beans, sun-dried tomatoes, rosemary, salt, dill seed, tamari, and vinegar. Puree to fully incorporate. Add the rice and about half of the pecans and pulse just to combine; do not fully puree or the rice will become too sticky. Add the oats and pulse just once or twice. Crush or chop the remaining pecans. Remove the blade from the food processor and add the remaining pecans, mixing by hand to incorporate. Place the bowl of the processor in the fridge and chill the mixture for about 30 minutes, if possible (this will firm up the mixture, which will help you shape it into patties).

Preheat a nonstick skillet over medium-high heat. Take scoops of the mixture (roughly ½ cup) and shape by hand into 11 or 12 patties. Working in batches, cook the patties for 5–7 minutes on the first side, then flip to cook the other side for 4–6 minutes. Once golden brown on both sides, remove and serve!

Garlic Note: The garlic in these burgers will not be cooked other than the cooking of the patties themselves. The raw garlic flavor can be strong for some, so judge how much garlic you want to use. One medium-large clove is usually enough flavor and garlic intensity—unless you really love more! If you want to substitute garlic powder, use about 1 teaspoon.

Sun-Dried Tomato Note: If possible, use sun-dried tomatoes that are loose (rather than packed in oil). If you have only oil-packed tomatoes, rinse and dry them well before using.

Dill Seed Note: If you don't have dill seed, you can try cumin seed. Do not substitute dry or fresh dill weed here. If you know you enjoy the flavor of dill seed, use a full teaspoon!

Nut-Free Note: I really like the flavor of toasted pecans here. However, you can also try toasted walnuts or, for a nut-free version, toasted pumpkin seeds.

Processor Note: A 16-cup food processor can manage this batch well. With 12- or 14-cup processors, you will want to remove some of the beet-carrot mixture before moving ahead and work in a couple of batches, up until adding the pecans. You can also work in batches the whole way, then crush the pecans separately and mix in by hand. Be sure to process thoroughly if working in batches to ensure the patties hold together well.

Advance Prep: If you want to prep these a day in advance, go for it! You can either keep the full mixture in a covered bowl in the refrigerator to shape when ready, or shape the patties in advance. These patties also freeze well—see the Kind Kitchen FAQ (page 23).

> **Recipe Renewal!** If you have any leftover burgers:
> - Break them up and serve as a Buddha bowl with a hot grain, steamed greens or other vegetables, and Buddha Dressing (page 67)!
> - Use in sandwiches, with a spread of hummus or nut cheese and sliced veggies and avocado.

Porto Burgers

A good portobello burger should be in every plant-based cook's repertoire. They are easy to make and very versatile, as they pair well with different seasonings. Plus, you can enjoy so many different toppings with them, it can be like a whole new burger every time!

Serves 3–4

2 tablespoons tamari

1 tablespoon ketchup

2 teaspoons Dijon mustard

2 teaspoons red wine vinegar or apple cider vinegar

½ teaspoon onion powder or garlic powder

½ teaspoon smoked paprika or more onion/garlic powder

1 tablespoon chopped fresh thyme or oregano (see note)

1 tablespoon chopped fresh chives (optional)

6–8 portobello mushrooms (wiped clean and gills removed; see note)

Couple pinches salt and pepper

In a very large bowl, combine the tamari, ketchup, mustard, vinegar, onion powder, paprika, and chopped fresh herbs and whisk together. Add the mushroom caps and move through the marinade to coat as best you can. Let the mushrooms marinate for 30 minutes or more, mixing once or twice during that time.

To grill: Preheat the grill to high or medium-high heat. Place the mushrooms on the grill and sprinkle on a pinch of salt and pepper. Grill for 5 to 7 minutes on the first side, until grill marks have formed. Turn the caps and grill for another 4 to 5 minutes, until cooked through.

To broil: Position an oven rack toward the top of the oven and set the oven to broil. Line a rimmed baking sheet with aluminum foil, then place a smaller lining of parchment paper on top of the foil—enough to cook the mushrooms on, but ensuring no parchment is extending beyond the edges of the pan (to prevent the parchment from burning). Place the caps on the prepared baking sheet. Broil for 8–10 minutes, until beginning to brown and soften and release juices, then flip and broil on the other side for 5–6 minutes, until browned and tender. The cooking time will depend on your oven and how close the mushrooms are to the broiling element.

Herb Note: Fresh herbs work better here than dried. If you don't have any, instead try other seasonings like ground spices (such as chili powder, more onion/garlic powder, or smoked paprika), or use more chopped chives or 1–2 tablespoons minced shallot or onion.

Mushroom Note: Portobello mushrooms can vary in size; if yours are very large, opt for 6 rather than 8 so the marinade will coat the caps well. To clean the mushrooms, remove the stems (reserve and trim to use in the marinade, or discard). Wipe the mushroom caps with a damp towel or paper towel (do not soak or rinse the caps). Use a large spoon to scrape the gills from the undersides of the caps, discarding the scrapings.

Serving Suggestions: Get creative with serving ideas here! Because these burgers are juicy and not heavy like a bean or grain-based burger, they are great in traditional burger buns. They're also lovely in whole-grain tortillas. Hearty toppings like nut cheese, bean spreads, and slices of avocado are really good!

Bistro Burgers

Many veggie burgers are bean-based, but sometimes we don't have beans on hand or are simply not able to consume them for a dietary reason. These grain-based burgers are bean-free but lack nothing in flavor or texture. They're stellar!

Makes about 10 patties; serves 4–5

1 cup chopped red bell pepper

½ cup sun-dried tomatoes (not packed in oil)

1 medium-large clove garlic

3–4 tablespoons nutritional yeast (see note)

3–4 tablespoons dried onion flakes

1 cup pumpkin seeds, plus ¼ cup crushed pumpkin seeds for optional coating

2 teaspoons smoked paprika

1 teaspoon dried rosemary leaves

½ teaspoon cumin seed and/or dill seed

Couple pinches sea salt

Freshly ground black pepper to taste

2 tablespoons mild miso

1 tablespoon tahini

1½ teaspoons Dijon mustard

1½ teaspoons red wine vinegar

1 cup frozen corn kernels

2 cups cooked sticky or short-grain brown rice, cooled (see note)

½ cup rolled oats (see note)

In the bowl of a large food processor, combine the bell pepper, sun-dried tomatoes, garlic, nutritional yeast, and onion flakes. Process for a minute to break up and begin to mince. Add the pumpkin seeds, smoked paprika, rosemary, cumin/dill seed, salt, pepper, miso, tahini, mustard, and vinegar. Process again for a minute, until the seeds are crumbly and becoming a bit sticky. Add the corn kernels and process briefly, then add the rice and oats. Pulse until the mixture holds together, using a spatula to scrape down the processor bowl as needed. Remove the food processor blade.

Take scoops of the mixture (roughly ½ cup) and shape by hand into about 10 patties.

Preheat a nonstick skillet over medium-high heat. If desired, spread the crushed ¼ cup pumpkin seeds on a plate. Dredge the patties in the crushed pumpkin seeds and turn to lightly coat both sides. Working in batches, cook the patties for 5–7 minutes on the first side, then flip to cook the other side for 4–6 minutes, until golden brown on both sides.

Nutritional Yeast Note: There isn't really a substitute for nooch. If you aren't able to use it, you can omit it or enhance the flavor of the burgers with another 1 tablespoon onion flakes or sun-dried tomatoes.

Rice Note: If you use a sticky rice, the patties will hold together a little better than if you use a long-grain rice—but either variety can be used.

Oat Note: Oats help absorb moisture in the burgers and help them hold. Instead of oats, you can substitute another ½–¾ cup rice or ½ cup whole-grain breadcrumbs.

Cooking Note: If you want to bake these in the oven, preheat the oven to 400°F. Place the patties on a rimmed baking sheet lined with parchment paper. Bake for about 20 minutes, turning the patties after about 10 minutes.

Thai Green Pea Patties with Mandarin Sweet 'n' Sour Sauce

These Thai curry patties are a little surprising—in a delightful way! Easy to prepare, they have a wonderful aromatic essence, great flavor, and pleasing texture.

Makes 10–11 patties and about ⅔ cup sauce; serves 3–4

Patties

1 cup frozen green peas, divided

1 small-medium clove garlic, peeled

1 tablespoon fresh lime or lemon juice

1½ tablespoons Thai curry paste (red, yellow, or green)

2½ cups cooked short-grain brown rice, cooled

½ teaspoon salt

Freshly ground black pepper to taste

½ cup rolled oats

⅓ cup fresh cilantro or basil (optional; do not substitute dried)

Mandarin Sweet 'n' Sour Sauce

1 teaspoon arrowroot powder

¼ teaspoon crushed red pepper (optional)

¼ cup pure maple syrup, date syrup, or coconut nectar

3–3½ tablespoons apple cider vinegar or rice vinegar

1 tablespoon tamari

¼–⅓ cup sliced or diced mandarin oranges or regular oranges

1–1½ tablespoons canned coconut milk (optional; see note)

Preheat the oven to 400°F. Line a rimmed baking sheet with parchment paper.

Combine about half of the green peas, the garlic, and lime juice in a food processor. Pulse several times to break up the garlic and peas. Add the Thai curry paste, rice, salt, and pepper and pulse until the mixture starts to come together. Add the oats, fresh herbs (if using), and remaining green peas and pulse to combine. Remove the blade from the processor bowl.

Take scoops of the mixture (about ½ cup) and place them on the prepared baking sheet. Flatten the patties lightly with a spatula. Bake for 10 minutes, then carefully flip and bake for another 6–8 minutes, until a little golden on each side.

Meanwhile, make the sauce. Whisk together the arrowroot, crushed red pepper (if using), syrup, vinegar (starting with 3 tablespoons), and tamari in a saucepan. Turn the heat to high and bring the mixture to a boil, whisking. Turn off the heat. Stir in the mandarins and remove the pan from the heat. Taste and add extra vinegar if you like. For a touch of smooth richness, add the coconut milk. Stir, then transfer the sauce to a serving bowl. Serve warm or let cool slightly.

Serving Suggestion: Try serving along with a side of broiled or steamed green beans or broccoli, or a green salad. A simple tofu or tempeh dish alongside is also a great pairing.

Sauce Note: if you want to skip the step of making a sauce, feel free to serve these patties with a prepared sweet chili sauce or your favorite prepared sweet 'n' sour sauce.

Coconut Milk Note: This sauce is delicious without the coconut milk. It does add just a touch of richness, so if you have an opened can of coconut milk in the fridge, give it a try!

Zucchini Fritters

I created this recipe when we were growing our own zucchini one year. Now, those zucchini can't grow fast enough to keep up with how much we love this recipe! Whether you opt for yellow or green, you don't need to peel the zucchini for this recipe; simply grate on the large holes of a box grater, or feed through the grating blade of a food processor.

Makes 7–8 fritters, serving 3 as a light meal or more as an appetizer (see note)

1 tablespoon fresh lemon juice

1 tablespoon tahini

3 cups grated zucchini

¾–1 cup chickpea flour (see note)

3–4 tablespoons chives or sliced green onions (green portion only)

½ teaspoon salt

½ teaspoon dill seed (see note)

Freshly ground black pepper to taste

1 teaspoon Dijon mustard (optional)

Stir together the lemon juice and tahini. In a large bowl, combine all the remaining ingredients and pour the lemon-tahini mixture on top. Combine with a spoon or spatula until you have a uniform mixture. As the zucchini releases moisture (from the added salt), the chickpea flour will absorb that liquid. Allow the mixture to sit for 15–20 minutes.

Heat a nonstick skillet over medium-high heat. Scoop a portion of the mixture (about ¼ cup), and transfer to your skillet. Use a spatula to flatten into a fritter shape. Depending on the size of your pan, you should be able to cook all the fritters in two batches. Cook on one side for 3–4 minutes, until golden. Flip and cook for another 2–4 minutes on the second side, until golden and cooked through. If the fritters are browning too quickly, reduce the heat to allow the centers to cook more fully.

Flour Note: Depending on the moisture in the zucchini, and how it measures grated, you may need more/less flour. I like ¾ cup; it yields fritters that are still moist with the zucchini but hold together just fine. You can always start with ¾ cup and adjust with a touch more flour if you like as you start to cook. More flour will yield firmer patties.

Dill Seed Note: Dill seed beautifully accents these fritters. If you don't have it, I wouldn't substitute fresh or dried dill weed. Instead, try substituting ¼–½ teaspoon cumin seed or fennel seed.

Serving Suggestions: These make a light meal or a lovely side dish. Serve with a vegan sour cream (or a nut cheese thinned with a little water), or even simply with ketchup or a balsamic reduction.

Appetizer Note: Shape these into smaller fritters for appetizer or nibbler portions. You can serve each with a small dollop of vegan sour cream or a drizzle of a balsamic reduction.

Seasoned Potato Squashers

Potatoes get a little more fun when squashed! To soften the potatoes for squashing, they can be baked or boiled.

Serves 4

3 pounds yellow or red potatoes or baby/new potatoes (see note)

¼–½ teaspoon sea salt, divided

½ teaspoon smoked paprika, divided (see note)

½–1 tablespoon nutritional yeast, divided (optional)

Freshly ground black pepper, divided (optional)

Few pinches minced fresh herbs (rosemary, thyme, chives, parsley), for garnish (optional)

To bake: Preheat the oven to 425°F. Pierce each potato with a fork or sharp knife. Place the potatoes on a rimmed baking sheet (for small potatoes) or directly on the middle oven rack (for larger potatoes). Bake for 40–50 minutes or even a little longer (depending on the potato size), until fully cooked. Remove from the oven and let cool slightly or fully.

To boil: Put the potatoes in a large pot and add water just to cover. Bring to a boil, then reduce the heat to a low-medium boil. Let cook for about 20–30 minutes, until fork-tender. Drain and let cool.

Get ready to "squash"! Heat the oven to 450°F and line a rimmed baking sheet with parchment paper. Spread out the potatoes on the baking sheet. Use a spatula, large fork, or the bottom of a mug to press and squish the potatoes, allowing the insides to burst through the skins and flatten on the sheet to ¼–½ inch thick. Sprinkle with about half of the seasonings. Bake for 9–10 minutes on one side, until a little golden. Flip, sprinkle on the remaining seasonings, and bake another 9–10 minutes or so, until crispy and golden. Taste and, if you'd like extra seasonings, add as desired. Garnish with fresh herbs, if using.

Potato Note: If you are steaming larger potatoes, you can halve them for quicker cooking. Smaller potatoes or new/baby potatoes can be kept whole. I don't recommend russet potatoes for this recipe.

Smoked Paprika Note: Smoked paprika has such robust flavor, much more than regular paprika. If you have only regular paprika, feel free to use it. Other seasonings can be used on these potatoes—whatever you love! For instance, try chili powder, garlic or onion powder, seasoned salt and pepper blends (such as truffle salt or lemon pepper), or salt-free seasonings.

Potato Chipz

You might want to eat the full batch of these nibbly chips yourself! Try them over dinner salads or soup.

Serves 3–4

¼ teaspoon coarse sea salt, divided

3 pounds red or Yukon Gold potatoes

2 tablespoons canned coconut milk

2 teaspoons fresh lemon juice

½ teaspoon smoked paprika (see note)

Preheat the oven to 400°F. Line a rimmed baking sheet with parchment paper, and sprinkle on a pinch of the salt. Slice the potatoes very thinly (about ⅛ inch), either using the slicing blade of a food processor or by hand with a knife or mandoline. Transfer the slices to a large bowl. Toss with the coconut milk, lemon juice, and smoked paprika. Spread out on the prepared baking sheet, spacing well. Sprinkle with the remaining salt. Bake for 30 minutes, then use a spatula to flip and move the potato slices around the pan to evenly cook. Bake for another 25–30 minutes, tossing the potatoes once or twice, until they are golden and crispy in spots. Season with extra salt or other seasonings to taste.

Paprika Note: Smoked paprika offers a much nicer flavor profile than regular paprika for these chipz. Other ideas for seasonings include ¼ teaspoon garlic or onion powder or ½ teaspoon chopped fresh rosemary.

Chipotle Chickpea Fries

My family absolutely loves these fries. They dig in and clamor for the last ones! If you're making them for younger kids, you may want to reduce the chipotle seasoning. These might replace your potato home fries!

Serves 2–3

1 cup chickpea (garbanzo bean) flour

2 cups water, divided

1 tablespoon nutritional yeast

½ teaspoon smoked paprika

¼–½ teaspoon ground turmeric

¼ teaspoon ground cumin

¼ teaspoon (rounded) salt

½ teaspoon agar powder (optional; see note)

1½–2½ teaspoons chipotle hot sauce (see note)

½ teaspoon pure maple syrup

For Coating

1 tablespoon fine cornmeal or corn flour

Few pinches sea salt and smoked paprika

Prepare an 8-inch square baking dish with a light wipe or spray of oil. Line the bottom and two sides with parchment paper for easy removal.

In a large saucepan, combine the chickpea flour with about half of the water, whisking until smooth. Add the remaining water and the other ingredients (except the coating). Place the saucepan over medium heat and bring to a boil, whisking frequently. Reduce the heat to low and continue to whisk for a couple of minutes as the mixture thickens. As it does, remove the whisk and use a spatula to continue to stir the mixture until fully thickened, for another minute or two.

Transfer the mixture to the prepared baking dish. Smooth the top and place the dish in the fridge to chill and set completely, at least 1 hour.

Preheat the oven to 450°F. Line a rimmed baking sheet with parchment paper. Sprinkle the parchment with the cornmeal and a few pinches of salt and smoked paprika. Remove the set chickpea mixture from the baking dish by lifting the edges of the parchment. Cut the block into "fries," ½–¾ inch thick, and then slice in half or thirds. Place the fries on the prepared baking sheet and gently turn to coat in the seasoning. Bake for 23–25 minutes, or longer if needed, until the fries are golden and slightly crispy. Move the fries around once during baking, as the fries around the edge of the pan tend to cook more quickly.

Agar Note: I like the texture the agar gives these fries, but if you don't have it, you can simply omit it.

Chipotle Note: I don't like things overly spicy, so I use about 1 teaspoon chipotle hot sauce for just a hint of heat and good flavor. If you want to kick up the heat, use 2 teaspoons or more.

Serving Suggestions: Pair with Sassy Sour Cream (page 103) or What-amole (page 104).

Baked Onion Rings

Crispy, crunchy, and munchy, these onion rings are so irresistible, it's hard to believe they aren't fried.

Serves 2–3

1 large or 2 medium onions, cut into ¼–½-inch rings (see note)

⅓ cup chickpea (garbanzo bean) flour

½ teaspoon sea salt, plus a couple pinches

½–¾ cup aquafaba (see note on page 24)

1–1½ cups panko or other breadcrumbs of choice

½ teaspoon smoked paprika or regular paprika

Submerge the onions in a large bowl of ice-cold water. Soak the onions for about 30 minutes.

Position your oven racks in the top and bottom thirds of your oven and preheat the oven to 450°F. Line 2 rimmed baking sheets with parchment paper.

Drain the onions and pat them dry with paper towels. Get your onion ring coating stations ready: Put the chickpea flour and a couple pinches of salt in a resealable plastic bag. Pour the aquafaba into a shallow bowl. Combine the breadcrumbs, ½ teaspoon salt, and paprika in another shallow bowl and stir to mix thoroughly, then transfer half of the crumb mixture to a separate shallow bowl. (The onion rings will be coated in three steps—first in the chickpea flour, then in the chickpea brine, and finally in the breadcrumbs. Separating the breadcrumbs into two batches will help keep them dry so they will adhere better to the onion rings. So, you will work with one bowl of breadcrumbs and then about halfway through the coating process, move on to that second bowl of breadcrumbs.)

Place the onions in the plastic bag, seal, and shake to coat the rings in the flour. Remove, and dip each ring first in the aquafaba, and next into the breadcrumb mixture. Place the coated rings on the prepared baking sheets. When you have coated all the rings, discard any extra aquafaba and breadcrumbs. Bake for 15 minutes, then flip the rings, swap the baking sheets from bottom to top, and bake for another 10–15 minutes, until golden and crispy.

Onion Note: Any variety of onion can be used; the flavor will be a little milder if you use a sweet onion.

Serving Suggestions: Serve with your favorite dressing, dipping sauce, natural ketchup, or a creamy sauce like Sassy Sour Cream (page 103).

Mamma Mia! Marinara

When you cook more from scratch, you notice how fresh and real simple food can taste. If you are tiring of jarred pasta sauces, try this marinara. Warning: its big flavor and fast cook time (courtesy of the pressure cooker!) might spoil you from ever going back to store-bought.

Makes 7–8 cups

¼ cup dry red or white wine *or* 2–3 tablespoons water or cranberry juice

2½ cups roughly chopped onion

1¼ teaspoons salt (or more to taste)

Freshly ground black pepper to taste

3 pounds tomatoes, roughly chopped (8–9 cups; see note)

¼–⅓ cup sun-dried tomatoes (not packed in oil), roughly chopped or sliced

5 large cloves garlic, quartered or roughly chopped

2–3 pitted dates, sliced (see note)

1–1½ cups loosely packed fresh basil (see note)

3–4 tablespoons fresh oregano leaves (see note)

Few pinches crushed red pepper (optional)

Set a multifunction pressure cooker (such as an Instant Pot) to sauté. Pour the wine into the pot and add the onion, salt, and pepper. Cook, stirring occasionally, 4–5 minutes, until the onion is slightly soft. Turn off the sauté function, then add the fresh tomatoes, sun-dried tomatoes, garlic, dates, basil, oregano, and crushed red pepper (if using).

Secure the lid and set the valve to the "sealed" position. Press the Manual button, then set the cook time for 20 minutes at high pressure. Allow the pot to come to pressure and cook. Once the timer goes, off, manually release the pressure or let it release naturally. Use an immersion blender to puree the sauce to the desired consistency. Taste and add extra salt, pepper, or sweetener if needed.

Tomato Note: I like Roma tomatoes here, but you can use any tomatoes you like. Tomatoes will be naturally sweeter and more flavorful in the summer. So, if you're making this off-season, you may need to adjust the salt and add a touch more dates or sweetener to taste. If you don't have great fresh tomatoes on hand, you can substitute two 28-ounce cans whole tomatoes.

Date Note: After cooking, you may want to add a touch more sweetener if your tomatoes are not naturally that sweet. If you need a touch more after pureeing, you can add a teaspoon or so of pure maple syrup, date syrup, date sugar, or coconut sugar.

Herb Note: Fresh herbs make a big flavor difference in this marinara. When tomatoes are in season, so is basil, so it's a natural pairing. If you don't have basil, you can use a little more fresh oregano (1–2 tablespoons) or some fresh thyme (2 tablespoons) or fresh rosemary (1–2 teaspoons). Fresh parsley can also be used, but it doesn't add as much flavor.

Chopping Note: Since this sauce will be pureed after cooking, there isn't any need to finely chop the vegetables. Just quickly chop in pieces, and into the pot they go!

Stovetop Method: If you don't have a pressure cooker, you can prepare this sauce on the stovetop. To do so, put the wine, onion, salt, and pepper in a large pot and set over high heat. Cook for 5–6 minutes, stirring occasionally, until the onion is soft. Add the fresh tomatoes, sun-dried tomatoes, garlic, dates, basil, oregano, and crushed red pepper (if using). Bring the mixture to a boil, stirring frequently. Reduce the heat to medium-low, cover, and simmer for 40 minutes. Use an immersion blender to puree the sauce to the desired consistency. Add extra salt, pepper, and/or sweetener to taste.

> **Recipe Renewal!**
> - Make a marinara pasta salad by combining cooked cooled pasta with some leftover sauce, sliced or chopped olives or capers, diced veggies of choice, and cooked beans or chopped tofu.
> - Freeze and use in Lofty Lasagna (page 161) later on!

The Ulti-Mac

I have made quite a few vegan mac 'n' cheese recipes over the years. This one blew my family's minds when we first tasted it. It's not just dairy-free but also nut-free—yet unbelievably luscious and rich. It's the ultimate mac 'n' cheese experience!

Serves 5–6

1–1¼ pounds dry pasta (see note)

1 cup cooked red or Yukon Gold potato flesh, cooled (see note)

½ cup raw unsalted sunflower seeds

½ cup rolled oats

1 teaspoon sea salt

1 medium clove garlic, peeled

¼ cup refrigerated canned coconut cream (see note)

3 tablespoons fresh lemon juice

1 tablespoon chickpea or other mild miso (optional; see note)

1 tablespoon tahini

2½ cups plain unsweetened nondairy milk, divided (see note)

½ cup water

¼–⅓ cup Ma-mesan (page 86; optional)

Preheat the oven to 400°F.

Bring a large pot of water to a boil and cook the pasta according to the package directions, keeping the pasta a little firm to the bite (it will cook further in the casserole).

Meanwhile, prepare the sauce. Combine the potato, sunflower seeds, oats, salt, garlic, coconut cream, lemon juice, miso (if using), tahini, and 1 cup of the milk in a blender. Puree until the potatoes and seeds begin to break down. Add another cup of milk and puree again until the mixture is fully smooth. Add the remaining milk and the water and puree again. The mixture should be silky smooth, without any texture from the seeds or oats.

Drain the pasta and transfer it to a 13 × 9-inch baking dish. Pour the prepared sauce over the noodles and gently stir to coat all the pasta. Sprinkle on the Ma-mesan (if using). Cover the pan with aluminum foil and bake for 25 minutes, then remove the foil. Set the oven to broil and broil for 3–5 minutes to lightly brown the top.

Pasta Note: If you like your mac bake extra saucy, use the lesser amount of pasta. The sauce will thicken with baking, and the pasta will absorb the sauce as it cooks as well.

Potato Note: It's helpful to batch-cook your potatoes in advance and have them on hand in the fridge.

Coconut Cream Note: Coconut milk adds a velvety, rich texture here, and the sweetness helps balance the bitter flavor of the seeds. Use regular (not light) coconut milk in this recipe. Before using, refrigerate the can overnight or for a few days. The thick cream will rise to the top and be easy to scoop and measure. Use only the thick cream (reserve the thin coconut milk for another use).

Miso Note: I enjoy chickpea miso for its light color and flavor, but you can use a mild-flavored soy-based miso, or omit it entirely.

Milk Note: Organic soy and oat milk are good flavor choices for this recipe.

Lofty Lasagna

Lasagna can seem difficult to make because there are a lot of steps! I resisted recording a recipe for so long for just that reason. Don't be intimidated by all the notes (okay, many of my recipes have lots of notes!): at its heart, this is a simple recipe that you can customize and put in regular rotation in your home!

Serves 6 or more

1 (1-pound) package lasagna noodles (see note)

3–4 cups sliced zucchini

Few pinches salt and freshly ground black pepper, or salt-free seasoning

1 (28-ounce) can tomato puree (see note)

1 batch Rustic Ricotta (page 163)

1½ cups sliced or cubed cooked sweet potato, cooled (see note)

1–2 tablespoons chopped fresh oregano *or* ⅓ cup fresh basil leaves or ⅓ cup Ma-mesan (page 86)

Preheat the oven to 375°F.

Bring a large pot of water to a boil and cook the lasagna noodles according to the package directions until al dente (err on the side of undercooking). Drain the pasta, then fill the pot with cold water and add the pasta back to the pot to help prevent it from cooking further.

Preheat a nonstick frying pan or grill pan over high heat for a couple of minutes. Once hot, add the zucchini slices and sprinkle with salt and pepper or salt-free seasoning. Sear for 3–4 minutes without moving them. Stir or flip the zucchini and sear for another 2–3 minutes (don't cook fully, just get a sear). Remove from the heat and set aside.

To assemble the lasagna, pour about ¾ cup of the tomato puree into the bottom of a 13 × 9-inch baking dish. Place 3–4 noodles over the sauce to cover, overlapping the noodles slightly if you like. Next, dollop about half of the ricotta over the noodles. You can try to spread it out to distribute evenly, or leave it more "rustic" in dollops—don't fret the prep!

Add another layer of noodles and top with about ¾ cup of the tomato puree. Distribute the seared zucchini more or less evenly over the top.

Add another layer of noodles. Dollop on the remaining ricotta and distribute the sweet potato over the ricotta. (Again, it doesn't have to be perfectly even!)

Add the last layer of noodles. If you have more than 3–4 noodles left, simply overlap and make a thicker top layer. Pour on the remaining tomato puree to generously cover the top layer of noodles. If you like, sprinkle with fresh herbs or parm.

Cover the dish with a layer of parchment paper first (so the top layer doesn't stick), then cover fully with aluminum foil. Bake for 45–50 minutes, removing the foil and parchment cover for the last 5–7 minutes to let the top brown slightly. Let rest for at least 10 minutes before slicing and serving.

Lasagna Noodle Note: You can use oven-ready noodles if you prefer and skip the boiling/soaking steps. They do require extra sauce, though, so use at least another 1 cup of puree or puree plus water—see below.

Tomato Puree Note: Store-bought pasta sauce is convenient but can overwhelm the flavors in lasagna. I use tomato puree (may be labeled as passata di pomodoro), which is simply tomatoes and sometimes salt. The simple, pure taste of the tomatoes lets the other components of the lasagna shine! Check the label; if it isn't seasoned, add a few pinches of sea salt to taste. You can also add freshly ground black pepper, a few tablespoons of chopped fresh oregano and basil, or a few pinches of dried basil and oregano or Italian seasoning. If your can contains less than 3 cups (the type I typically buy has about 2½ cups) and you don't have any other puree, you can "stretch" it with water. After you first pour ¾ cup puree into the lasagna dish, simply add about ½ cup water to the can and stir to mix it in. Of course you can also make up the difference with jarred pasta sauce if you have it on hand.

Sweet Potato Note: Since I batch-cook sweet potatoes (see page 11), they are ready to layer in this lasagna. If you don't have sweet potatoes prebaked, instead peel and slice raw sweet potatoes, then cook (pan-fry, bake, or steam) until tender to use in this recipe.

Other Vegetable Options: Mix 'n' match other veggies instead of or in addition to the zucchini and sweet potato in this recipe. Try:
- 1 pound mushrooms, cleaned and chopped—place on a baking sheet, drizzle with 2 teaspoons balsamic reduction, sprinkle with ¼ teaspoon salt and freshly ground black pepper to taste; broil for 8–10 minutes, tossing occasionally to brown
- 2 cups chopped baby spinach leaves plus 1 tablespoon chopped fresh oregano or ¼ cup chopped fresh basil
- 1 cup chopped or sliced roasted red bell peppers
- 1½ cups broken or chopped canned or jarred artichoke hearts

Rustic Ricotta

This ricotta has a mellow flavor and bakes up beautifully. Try it in my Lofty Lasagna (page 161) or in stuffed shell pasta dishes.

Makes about 2 cups

1 (12–16-ounce) package medium-firm tofu, squeezed to remove water, divided (see note)

1 cup soaked raw cashews or ¾ cup soaked raw sunflower seeds (see page 12)

2 tablespoons chopped fresh chives (optional)

1½ tablespoons nutritional yeast

¾ teaspoon sea salt

Couple pinches ground nutmeg

2 tablespoons fresh lemon juice

1 tablespoon mild miso

1 teaspoon red wine vinegar

½ teaspoon pure maple syrup

In the bowl of a food processor, combine about half of the tofu with the remaining ingredients. Puree until very smooth. Add the remaining tofu and pulse a couple of times to lend a slight chunky consistency to the ricotta. Use right away or store in an airtight container in the refrigerator for up to 4 days.

Tofu Note: If you are able to press the tofu for 10–20 minutes in advance, it's helpful to remove some of the excess water. If not, use several paper towels or a tea towel to squeeze out as much water as you can.

1-Minute Pasta Alfredo

Okay, okay, from start to finish this will take you a bit longer than that to prepare—but the pressure-cooking time is just 1 minute! Plus, you can begin the base of the sauce earlier in the day if you need to, then add the pasta when ready to cook it up. Get ready for fast comfort food!

Serves 4–5

⅓ cup dry white wine or water

2 tablespoons raw tahini or cashew butter (not roasted)

3 tablespoons refrigerated canned coconut cream (see note)

1 tablespoon potato flour or another flour

1 teaspoon sea salt

Few pinches ground nutmeg

Freshly ground black pepper to taste

2–3 cloves garlic, minced or grated

2½ cups hot or boiling water, divided

4½ cups plain unsweetened nondairy milk (see note)

2–3 tablespoons nutritional yeast

1 pound dry pasta (see note)

1 tablespoon fresh lemon juice, or more to taste

Minced fresh parsley or chives and/or Ma-mesan (page 86), for garnish (optional)

Set a multifunction pressure cooker (such as an Instant Pot) to sauté. Pour in the wine, tahini, coconut cream, and potato flour. As the heat comes up, whisk to work the ingredients together until smooth, then add the salt, nutmeg, pepper, garlic, and ½ cup of the water. Whisk again to incorporate the garlic and begin to cook it in the sauce. Whisk occasionally as the sauce thickens; it will take a minute or two. Then whisk in another 1½ cups water. Turn off the sauté function. Add the milk and nutritional yeast and stir.

Add the pasta (breaking up long pasta; see note) and stir. Secure the lid and set the valve to the "sealed" position. Press the Manual button, then set the cook time for 1 minute at high pressure. Allow the pot to come to pressure and cook. Once the timer goes off, turn off the pot and allow to sit for 1–2 minutes, then manually release pressure. Open the lid and check the pasta; if it needs more cooking time, return the lid and let sit for another couple of minutes. When ready, add the lemon juice and remaining ½ cup water and stir. Taste and add any additional seasonings as desired, and thin with more milk or water if needed. Serve, topped with herbs and/or parm, if you like!

Coconut Cream Note: A little bit of coconut cream adds an extra layer of creamy richness to this sauce. Use regular (not light) coconut milk in this recipe. Before using, refrigerate the can overnight or for a few days. The thick cream will rise to the top and be easy to scoop and measure. An alternative is plain unsweetened nondairy coffee creamer. That richness will go far in this pasta, and you could use ½ cup or more, substituting for some of the nondairy milk. (Don't use more than 2 tablespoons of coconut cream, however—the flavor becomes too pronounced in the sauce.)

Milk Note: I prefer organic soy or oat milk in this recipe. You can use another; just be sure it doesn't have a noticeable flavor that will overpower the other flavors (like hemp milk). If you don't have quite 4½ cups, substitute extra water, up to 1 cup.

Pasta Note: Which pasta to pick? Use any shape, such as a cut pasta (penne, fusilli) or a long noodle (spaghetti, fettuccine). In the Instant Pot, longer pasta can stick together more easily than cut pasta, so break into thirds and stir very well before bringing to pressure. You can use regular wheat pasta or another grain variety. (In testing, I did find brown rice pasta a little too "gummy," and the starches took over the viscosity of the sauce.)

Stovetop Method: In a large pot, combine the wine, tahini, coconut cream, and potato flour over medium-high heat. As the heat comes up in the pot, whisk to work the ingredients together until smooth. Reduce the heat to low, then add the salt, nutmeg, pepper, garlic, and ½ cup of the water. Whisk again to incorporate the garlic and begin to cook it in the sauce. Whisk occasionally as the sauce thickens; this will take a minute or two. Turn off the heat and stir in 3½ cups milk and the nooch.

Meanwhile, prepare the pasta in another pot according to the package directions and cook until just al dente, or even a little firmer. Drain well, and add the pasta to the pot with the Alfredo mixture. Turn up the heat to high. Once bubbling, reduce the heat and let simmer for a few minutes to finish cooking the pasta. If needed, add up to ¼ cup more milk. Once the pasta is just nicely cooked through, turn off the heat and add the lemon juice. Taste and adjust the seasonings as needed. Serve. (Note that as pasta sits, it will continue to thicken and absorb more of the liquid).

Awakened Pad Thai

This pad thai is so much better than takeout, with a nut- and peanut-free sauce and a fresher take on ingredients. It's more delicious than you might expect!

Serves 3

Sauce

3 tablespoons pumpkin seeds

3 tablespoons coconut sugar or date sugar

1 tablespoon peeled and roughly chopped fresh ginger

2–3 cloves garlic, sliced or chopped

⅓–½ cup water, divided

¼ cup tamari

2 tablespoons fresh lime juice

2 tablespoons tamarind concentrate *or* 1 tablespoon ketchup plus 1 tablespoon rice vinegar

1 tablespoon tahini

Dash hot sauce (see note)

Pasta and Veggies

8 ounces dry rice noodles, such as stick or vermicelli noodles

1 cup carrot matchsticks

4 green onions, sliced, white and green parts separated

½ cup thinly sliced zucchini

½ cup very thinly sliced red bell pepper

Pinch salt

1 cup cubed extra-firm tofu (about half of a 12-ounce package)

1 cup shredded or thinly sliced red cabbage or napa cabbage

⅓ cup chopped cilantro, plus more for serving

4 lime wedges

Hot sauce, for serving

In a blender, combine all the sauce ingredients, starting with about half of the water. Blend until the seeds are fully processed and the sauce is smooth. Add the remaining water and puree again. Set aside.

Cook the noodles according to the package directions. Once just tender or even before fully tender, drain and rinse briefly under cold water.

Heat a large pot over high heat. Put in the carrots, white parts of the green onions, zucchini, bell pepper, and salt. Toss for a minute in the hot pan to begin to sear. Reduce the heat to medium-low, add the sauce and cooked noodles, and toss until the noodles are heated through and coated evenly with the sauce. Add the tofu, cabbage, cilantro, and the green parts of the green onions. Toss just to heat through, then serve immediately with lime wedges, extra hot sauce, and extra cilantro if desired.

Hot Sauce Note: Even if you love hot sauce, start with a modest amount. There is a good kick in the sauce from the ginger and garlic, so it's best to use just a dash of hot sauce and then adjust when finishing the dish. You can always add more, but you can't take it away.

Serving Tip: Often when we serve a pasta dish it gets cold quickly—because our serving bowls are cold! Try warming your bowls in the oven or toaster oven on very low heat (175–200°F) for 5 minutes or more before serving up the pasta.

Luscious Avocado Pasta

This lusciously satisfying sauce can be prepped in minutes! It's also very kid-friendly, and you can easily adjust the seasonings, including basil, garlic, and pepper, to your personal tastes.

Serves 4

1 pound pasta of choice

1 cup avocado flesh (from 1½–2 small-medium avocados), plus ½–¾ cup cubed avocado

1 cup precooked Yukon Gold or red potato flesh, cooled

1 medium clove garlic, peeled

1 teaspoon sea salt

1½ cups water, or more to thin as desired

2½ tablespoons fresh lemon juice

1 tablespoon tahini or raw cashew butter

1 tablespoon chickpea miso or other mild miso

½ teaspoon Dijon mustard

½ teaspoon pure maple syrup

⅓–½ fresh cup basil leaves, plus more for garnish

½–1 teaspoon grated lemon zest

Salt and pepper to taste

Lemon wedges, for serving

Cook the pasta according to the package directions until just tender or a little al dente.

While the pasta cooks, in a blender, combine 1 cup of avocado flesh, the potato, garlic, salt, water, lemon juice, tahini, miso, mustard, and syrup. Puree until very smooth. If it's very thick and not pureeing, add more water as needed. Add the fresh basil and lemon zest and puree just briefly into the sauce.

Drain the cooked pasta. Pour the sauce into the pot and add back the pasta. Gently toss to warm the sauce and distribute through the pasta. If the sauce is too thick, add a splash of water and gently heat over a low setting for a couple of minutes. Taste and season with salt and/or pepper if desired. When ready to serve, add the cubed avocado and mix. Garnish with a sprinkling of basil and serve with lemon wedges.

Greek Koftas

Koftas are a type of Middle Eastern meatball, and often include seasonings like cumin seed, coriander, allspice, ginger, or mint. These are a Greek-inspired version—some vegan fusion food!

Serves 4–5, makes 25–30 balls

¼ cup pumpkin seeds

¼ cup sunflower seeds

¼ cup dry sun-dried tomatoes

1 medium-large clove garlic, peeled

⅔ cup chopped zucchini

⅓ cup fresh parsley leaves

2 teaspoons dried oregano

1½ teaspoons chopped fresh rosemary leaves or ½ teaspoon dried

¼ teaspoon ground allspice

¼ teaspoon sea salt

1½ teaspoons balsamic vinegar

2 cups cooked brown rice, cooled

½ cup rolled oats or ¾ cup breadcrumbs

½ cup sliced pitted green or kalamata olives (see note)

Preheat the oven to 375°F. Line a rimmed baking sheet with parchment paper.

In a food processor, combine the pumpkin seeds, sunflower seeds, sun-dried tomatoes, and garlic and pulse until crumbly. Add the zucchini, parsley, oregano, rosemary, allspice, salt, and vinegar and puree until the zucchini is broken down. Add the rice and oats and pulse to incorporate; do not fully process or the rice will become too sticky. The mixture should hold together when pressed with your fingers. Add the olives and just pulse in. Remove the blade from the processor.

For each kofta, scoop out 1–1½ tablespoons of the mixture and place on the baking sheet. Bake for 18–20 minutes, until dry to the touch and lightly golden.

Olive Note: Have family members who dislike olives? Form balls with about half of the batch, then add ¼ cup sliced olives to the remaining half-batch.

Serving Suggestions: Serve on pasta topped with your favorite tomato-based sauce, or try in a long sandwich bun like a meatball sub! Koftas are often served with pitas, salads, and dipping sauces—try them with the ranch version of my Creamy House Dressing (page 73) or Sassy Sour Cream (page 103). Leftovers can be used in sandwiches or to top lunch salad bowls.

Pumpkin Seed Pesto Pasta

I have made basil pesto with cashews, Brazil nuts, and pistachios (I prefer them all to pine nuts). But could a nut-free version equally impress? This one with nutrient-rich pumpkin seeds sure does!

Serves 4–5

¾ cup raw unsalted pumpkin seeds (see note), plus 1–2 tablespoons crushed pumpkin seeds for garnish

2 tablespoons nutritional yeast

1–2 medium-large cloves garlic, peeled (see note)

Freshly ground black pepper to taste

3½ tablespoons fresh lemon juice

2 tablespoons tahini

¾ teaspoon sea salt, plus more to taste (see note)

3 cups loosely packed fresh basil leaves, plus more for garnish

1 cup loosely packed spinach leaves

2–5 tablespoons water

½–1 teaspoon grated lemon zest

1 pound whole-grain pasta (see note)

Handful of sliced cherry or grape tomatoes (optional)

Lemon wedges, for serving

In a food processor, combine the pumpkin seeds, nutritional yeast, garlic, salt, pepper, lemon juice, and tahini. Process briefly to break up. Add the basil and spinach and process again. Depending on how dry the spinach and basil leaves are, you may need to add water at this stage to bring the puree together. Start with a tablespoon and puree again, adding more water as needed to reach a fairly smooth consistency. Once the pesto reaches your desired texture, add the lemon zest and pulse. (The pesto can be stored in the fridge in an airtight container for up to 4 days.)

Cook the pasta according to the package directions until al dente (almost fork-tender). Retain a small amount of the cooking water (¼ cup or so) and drain the pasta, but don't rinse (see note). Return the pasta to the pot and toss with your desired amount of pesto, plus a tablespoon at a time of the reserved cooking water, until the pasta is as saucy as you like. Season to taste with additional salt and pepper. Serve garnished with a sprinkle of crushed pumpkin seeds and basil, sliced tomatoes (if using), and lemon wedges.

Pumpkin Seed Note: I keep raw, sprouted pumpkin seeds (such as the Go Raw brand) on hand. Seasoned with just a touch of salt, they are fantastic for snacking—and to cook with! If you want to use them (in full or partially) in this recipe, omit the salt and season to taste after blending.

Garlic Note: Because the pesto is warmed by the pasta rather than cooked, the garlic maintains a raw taste, so I typically use just one garlic clove. If you love raw garlic, go for more!

Salt Note: You may want to add more salt to this pesto after tossing with the pasta; it depends on how much of the pesto you use. For instance, if you like just a light coating of pesto with your pasta, you may want a touch more salt. If you love a good dose of the pesto sauce, however, you may find it seasoned just enough.

Pasta Note: I always instruct "don't rinse the pasta" when working with a heated pasta dish. There's one exception: brown rice pasta. Brown rice pasta is especially sticky, so it's okay to give it a quick rinse. You can still keep some of the starchy cooking water to mix back into the pasta with the pesto.

Recipe Renewal! Store any leftover pesto separately from the pasta. To use up leftover pesto, try it . . .
- as a base on pizza with your favorite toppings (I like roasted red bell peppers, sliced pitted kalamata olives, halved cherry tomatoes, and thinly sliced red onion).
- as a filling for portobello mushroom caps! Remove the stems, chop, and mix into the pesto. Scrape the gills from the underside of the portobellos and discard. Fill each cap with an inch or so of pesto, add a sprinkling of seasoned breadcrumbs, and bake (at 425°F) until golden and tender. You can also use button mushrooms and serve as a side or appetizer.
- as a spread for sandwiches.
- mixed into rice for a lunch bowl.

Soulful Shepherd's Pie

This shepherd's pie is plenty hearty with spuds, lentils, and veggies. For the topping, I go with sweet potatoes instead of your standard mashed spuds. It's serious comfort food!

Serves 4–5

Base

¼ cup dry red wine

1–1½ cups diced yellow sweet potato or red/Yukon Gold potato (can use frozen)

1 cup diced onion

¼ cup steel-cut oats or buckwheat groats

2 teaspoons garlic powder

1½ teaspoons dried oregano

1 teaspoon smoked paprika (see note)

½ teaspoon celery seed (optional)

Pinch salt and freshly ground black pepper

¼ cup flour (any variety; I like either spelt or millet)

¼ cup tamari or 2 tablespoons tamari plus 2 tablespoons vegan Worcestershire sauce

1 cup water, divided

1 cup vegetable broth or more water

1½ tablespoons tomato paste or 2 tablespoons ketchup

2½–3 cups cooked French or green/brown lentils (see note)

1½ cups frozen vegetable medley (such as corn, peas, and carrots

Sweet Potato Topping

4 cups cooked peeled orange sweet potato flesh, cooled

1 tablespoon nutritional yeast

¼ teaspoon (generous) sea salt

⅓–½ cup plain unsweetened nondairy milk or water

1 tablespoon tahini (optional)

Preheat the oven to 400°F.

To prepare the base, in a large saucepan or skillet, combine the wine, potato, onion, oats, garlic powder, oregano, paprika, celery seed (if using), salt, and pepper. Cook over medium-high heat for 7–8 minutes, stirring frequently, until the onion is softening. If the pan becomes dry, add a splash of water. Add the flour and tamari and stir, then add a good splash from the 1 cup of water. Allow the mixture to come together and thicken. Add the remaining water, the broth, and tomato paste. Bring the mixture to a slow boil, then reduce the heat to low, cover, and simmer for 10 minutes, or until the potatoes are becoming tender.

Meanwhile, prepare the topping. Combine all the topping ingredients in a large bowl, starting with ⅓ cup milk. Use an immersion blender to puree. Alternatively, you can mash the sweet potatoes by hand; if using the tahini, first mix it with some of the milk to easily incorporate it. Add and blend in the additional milk if necessary to bring the topping to your desired consistency.

Remove the filling mixture from the heat and stir in the lentils and frozen vegetables. Transfer the lentil base to a 13 × 9-inch baking dish. Spread the sweet potato topping over the lentil base. It does not need to be perfectly smooth! Bake for 20–25 minutes, until the casserole is bubbling and the topping is a little golden. Remove from the oven and let sit for 5 minutes before serving.

Paprika Note: You can substitute regular paprika, but smoked gives more flavor.

Lentil Note: My favorite lentils to use in this recipe are the prepackaged cooked lentils from Trader Joe's. They have the perfect color and texture for this recipe. They do include some salt, so if cooking lentils from scratch, you might want to add a pinch of salt.

Quick-Fix Tip: I sometimes make this with a hash brown topping instead of the mashed sweet potato topping. It goes like this: Combine 6 cups frozen hash browns (or grated cooked potatoes), 3 tablespoons nutritional yeast, and ¼ teaspoon sea salt in a bowl. Spread the mixture over the lentil base in the baking dish and bake as directed.

Phyllo Phenom Rolls

Sometimes you want to prepare a main that feels a little fancier, something that works well for a dinner party or a holiday main. Phyllo pastry steps in to bring the wow factor. These rolls look impressive and taste phenomenal!

Makes 8 rolls

Vegetable Filling

1½ cups diced onion

2 teaspoons chopped fresh thyme

1 teaspoon chopped fresh rosemary

¾ teaspoon smoked or regular paprika

¾ teaspoon sea salt

½ teaspoon fennel seed (see spice note)

¼ teaspoon allspice

⅛ teaspoon ground nutmeg

Freshly ground black pepper

¼ cup dry white wine

3 cups diced zucchini (see note)

2 cups diced red, orange, or yellow bell pepper

2 medium-large cloves garlic, minced

1 cup cooked or canned (rinsed and drained) chickpeas

⅓ cup chopped pitted dates

Rolls

1 batch Truffle-Salted Nut Cheese (page 106; see spice note)

1 package (16 sheets) phyllo, thawed

4–6 tablespoons refrigerated canned coconut cream (see note)

Couple pinches smoked paprika and coarse salt for sprinkling

Few pinches fresh thyme

To prepare the vegetable filling, combine the onion, thyme, rosemary, paprika, salt, fennel seed, allspice, nutmeg, black pepper, and wine. Cook over medium-high heat for 3–4 minutes, until the onion begins to soften, then add the zucchini, bell pepper, garlic, and chickpeas. Reduce the heat to medium, stir, and cook for another 9–10 minutes, until the vegetables are tender. If the vegetables are sticking, add a splash of water. Turn off the heat, add the dates, and stir. Set the mixture aside to cool to room temperature before proceeding. (If you need to cool it quickly, transfer the mixture to a large plate or parchment-lined baking dish to hasten cooling.)

Preheat the oven to 400°F. Line a rimmed baking sheet with parchment paper and brush on a little coconut cream.

Place a lightly dampened dish towel over the phyllo sheets to keep them moist while preparing the rolls.

Cut the stack of phyllo sheets in half crosswise so you have two smaller rectangular stacks. To make each roll, take one rectangle and lightly brush the top with some of the coconut cream. Place another sheet on top, brush again, and another sheet, brushing again. Add a fourth sheet, but this time don't brush with coconut milk. Add 3–4 tablespoons of the nut cheese along the shorter length of the phyllo, spreading it out slightly with a butter knife and leaving an inch or two around the top edge and both sides. Then layer about 1 cup of the cooled veggie mixture on top of the nut cheese. You will roll the phyllo much like rolling a burrito: starting at the filled edge, tuck in the left and right edges as you roll up. Brush the finished roll with coconut cream and place on the prepared baking sheet.

Repeat the process to make a total of 8 rolls (you may have a little nut cheese left). Sprinkle a few pinches of smoked paprika and coarse sea salt on the tops of the finished rolls. Bake for 23–25 minutes, until golden brown. Serve warm with a sprinkle of fresh thyme.

Spice Note: I like using fennel seed in combination with the truffle essence in the nut cheese, but you can prepare the nut cheese seasoned simply with salt and without the truffle zest. If so, try cumin seed in the vegetable filling instead of fennel seed if desired.

Zucchini Note: If making this dish in the fall or winter, you might want to substitute winter squash for the zucchini. If using winter squash, add it with the onion. Cook with the onion until tender, this will take a few minutes longer than if using zucchini.

Coconut Cream Note: Use regular (not light) coconut milk in this recipe. Before using, refrigerate the can overnight or for a few days. The thick cream will rise to the top and be easy to scoop and measure. Use only the thick cream (reserve the thin coconut milk for another use).

Serving Suggestion: Serve these with a drizzle of Seasoned Balsamic Reduction, page 87.

Lentil and Sweet Potato Meatloaf

This loaf brings traditional savory flavors together with a hint of sweetness from the potatoes. It holds together well and is surprisingly easy to prep. With batch-cooking sweet potatoes (see page 11) and having lentils at the ready, the food processor takes care of the rest of the work!

Serves 5–6

2 cups cooked brown lentils, divided

1 cup cooked orange sweet potato flesh, cooled

½ cup cooked red or Yukon Gold potato flesh, cooled

1 medium-large clove garlic

3 tablespoons dried onion flakes

2 tablespoons flax meal

1 teaspoon dried oregano *or* 1 tablespoon fresh oregano leaves

½ teaspoon dried thyme *or* 1½ teaspoons fresh thyme leaves

½ teaspoon celery seed

Freshly ground black pepper to taste

¼ cup tomato paste

3 tablespoons tamari

1 tablespoon balsamic vinegar

1 tablespoon tahini

2 cups rolled oats

¼ cup pumpkin seeds

Topping Options

½ cup cooked sweet potato flesh

3–4 tablespoons ketchup and/or natural barbecue sauce

Salt and freshly ground black pepper to taste

Preheat the oven to 375°F. Spray or wipe a glass loaf pan with a smidgen of oil and line with parchment paper, letting the paper overhang the sides of the dish.

In a food processor, combine 1 cup of the lentils, the potatoes, garlic, onion flakes, flax meal, oregano, thyme, celery seed, pepper, tomato paste, tamari, vinegar, and tahini. Puree briefly, until fairly well combined but not completely smoothed out. Add the remaining 1 cup lentils, the oats, and the pumpkin seeds and pulse a couple of times, scraping down the sides of the bowl as needed, until the mixture is fairly well combined but still has texture—take care not to overprocess. Remove the blade and use a silicone spatula to mix a little more by hand.

Transfer the mixture to the prepared loaf pan. Smooth out with a spatula to evenly distribute the loaf in the dish. For the topping, you have a couple of options. You can mash the additional sweet potato and spread it over the top, then sprinkle with a few pinches of salt and pepper. Or, you can go with a more traditional topping of ketchup or barbecue sauce, spreading it on top with a spatula or brush.

Cover the dish with aluminum foil. Bake for 30 minutes, then remove the foil and bake for another 6–7 minutes, until the topping is set. Remove from the oven and let cool in the pan for 5–10 minutes. Lift the loaf out of the dish using the parchment. Slice and serve!

> **Recipe Renewal!** Leftover meatloaf?
> - Break up leftovers into bite-size pieces and roll into "meatballs." Bake at 375°F for 15 minutes, or until heated through and browning in spots (or another few minutes for a crispier texture), and serve with pasta.
> - Use in sandwiches or tortilla wraps for lunches.

Chickpea Satay Casserole

This peanut sauce is flavorful yet lightened with pureed fresh vegetables. Once the sauce is made, it's an easy dish to pull together with chickpeas and chopped vegetables. Bake and serve with rice, and dinner's done!

Serves 4–5

Peanut Sauce

½ cup roughly chopped carrot

½ cup roughly chopped red, yellow, or orange bell pepper

½ cup peeled roughly chopped zucchini or more carrot or bell pepper

1–2 cloves garlic, peeled

1 tablespoon peeled and chopped fresh ginger

1 tablespoon pure maple syrup or coconut/date sugar (optional)

⅛–¼ teaspoon crushed red pepper (optional; see note)

1 cup water, divided

¼–⅓ cup natural peanut butter (see note)

3 tablespoons tamari

2 tablespoons apple cider vinegar

2 tablespoons natural ketchup

Casserole

2 (14-ounce) cans chickpeas, rinsed and drained

2 cups small cubes red, yellow, or orange bell peppers

1 cup small cubes zucchini

1 cup chopped fresh or frozen green beans or more zucchini

Garnish (optional)

Chopped green onions

Chopped peanuts

Preheat the oven to 400°F.

In a blender, combine all the ingredients for the sauce, starting with ½ cup water. Puree until smooth, then add the remaining ½ cup water and puree again.

Pour the sauce into a 13 × 9-baking dish. Add the chickpeas, bell peppers, zucchini, and green beans and gently stir.

Cover the dish with aluminum foil and bake for 15 minutes. Remove the foil, stir well, re-cover with foil, and bake for another 10 minutes. Remove the foil and bake for a final 10 minutes, stirring once or twice during this time, until the sauce has thickened and the vegetables are tender. Garnish with green onions and peanuts, if desired.

Peanut Butter Note: You can use as little as ¼ cup in this sauce, but ⅓ cup will give you a richer taste. If you want to swap out peanut butter, try using almond butter or cashew butter—or, for a nut-free version, about half-and-half sunflower seed butter and tahini. Keep in mind that almond and cashew butters are naturally sweeter than peanut butter, and all are sweeter than seed butters. Taste the sauce after it begins to thicken and adjust with maple syrup if needed. Finally, do check that your nut butters don't already have sweeteners. If they do, you may not want any added sweetener.

Red Pepper Note: If you're serving this to kids or anyone who prefers a milder sauce, omit the crushed red pepper. You can serve individual portions with hot sauce for those who like the heat!

Serving Suggestions: Serve over a cooked grain like brown basmati rice, jasmine rice, quinoa, whole-wheat couscous, or millet. With a grain, this dish serves 5–6.

Recipe Renewal! Got leftovers?

- Mix rice into some of the leftover casserole and serve in a Buddha bowl with fresh or steamed greens, some fresh crunchy veg like chopped cucumbers or grated carrot, and a good dollop of mango chutney!
- Use the casserole for a twist on Stuffed Sweet Potatoes (page 192), spooning in the leftovers in place of the black beans, salsa, corn, and grains. After baking, drizzle on some Cilantro Lover's Dressing (page 71) or Ninja Dressing (page 70).

Quinoa-Lentil Stir-Fry

This is an example of how a little planning goes a long way in quick meal prep. When you batch-cook staples like quinoa and lentils (or even have store-bought lentils in your pantry), you can bring together a recipe like this in mere minutes!

Serves 4

Pinch sea salt

1 cup diced carrot

2–2½ cups chopped or torn broccoli florets

1 cup green onions, sliced, white and green parts separated

½ cup diced red, orange, or yellow bell pepper

1 medium clove garlic, grated or minced, *or* ½ teaspoon garlic powder

3½–4 cups cooked quinoa

1½ cups cooked brown or French lentils (see note)

⅔ cup frozen corn kernels

¼–⅓ cup tamari (see lentil note)

2–3 teaspoons water

Freshly ground black pepper to taste

Sprinkle a pinch of salt in a large wok or nonstick skillet with a lid (see note), add the carrot, cover, and cook over medium-high heat for 2–3 minutes, until the carrot starts to soften. Add the broccoli, the white parts of the green onions, the bell pepper, and garlic. Stir, cover again, and cook for 2–3 minutes, until the broccoli is just starting to turn a brighter green and the green onions are fragrant. Stir in the quinoa, lentils, corn, and tamari. Keeping the pan uncovered, cook for 4–5 minutes, stirring occasionally, until the vegetables are tender and heated through and still bright in color; add a couple teaspoons of water if the mixture is sticking. Add the green parts of the green onions and stir. Taste and season with salt and pepper, if desired.

Lentil Note: I love using the steamed French lentils that are in the refrigerated section of Trader Joe's. They have good flavor and texture, and help with quick meal prep. They can be kept frozen as well, and simply thawed in advance to use in this recipe. These lentils do contain salt, so don't add too much salt at the beginning when sautéing the veggies. Also, you can use a low-sodium tamari if using prepared lentils with salt.

Cooking Note: If you don't have a large enough wok or skillet, use two skillets. Alternatively, you can cook most of the stir-fry, reserving a portion of the lentils and quinoa, and then just add them when finishing.

Idea: Stir-fries are quite adaptable! You can substitute other vegetables that have similar cooking times and textures. For instance, try cauliflower in place of the broccoli, zucchini in place of the bell peppers, or frozen peas in place of the frozen corn.

Recipe Renewal!
- Mix leftovers with tomato sauce and reheat in the oven. Serve "sloppy joe" style in buns or pitas, with a green salad on the side.
- Use leftovers to bulk up a lunch bowl.
- Use leftovers in a lunch wrap with nut cheese or another spread.

Sweet 'n' Sour Lentils

Stovetop or pressure cooker, this is a pretty quick fix—and even better, it's a tasty fix! The sweet 'n' sour flavor works really well with lentils. Be sure to add the chopped cashews to the finished dish for extra texture!

Serves 4–5

2–3 tablespoons water plus
   2⅓ cups water, divided

1 cup chopped onion

¼ teaspoon sea salt, plus more to taste

1½ cups green, brown, or French lentils, rinsed

2 large cloves garlic, grated or minced

1 cup chopped carrot

1 cup chopped red bell pepper

⅛ teaspoon ground cloves

Freshly ground black pepper to taste

¼ cup tomato paste

¼ cup apple cider vinegar

2 tablespoons tamari or coconut aminos, plus more to taste

1½ tablespoons pure maple syrup or date syrup

½–¾ cup fresh or frozen pineapple cubes

⅓ cup crushed cashews or pumpkin seeds

To prepare in a multifunction pressure cooker (such as an Instant Pot): Set the cooker to sauté. Pour in the 2–3 tablespoons water, add the onion and salt, and cook for 4–5 minutes, stirring occasionally, until the onion has slightly softened. Turn off the sauté function. Add all the remaining ingredients except the pineapple and cashews and stir. Secure the lid and set the valve to the "sealed" position. Press the Manual button, then set the cook time for 12 minutes at high pressure. Allow the pot to come to pressure and cook. Once the timer goes off, turn off the pot and allow the pressure to naturally release. Stir in the pineapple and let sit for a few minutes to heat through. Taste and adjust the seasoning as desired. Serve topped with crushed cashews.

To prepare on the stovetop: Heat a medium saucepan over medium-high heat. Pour in the 2–3 tablespoons water and add the onion and salt. Cook for 4–5 minutes, stirring occasionally, until the onion has slightly softened. Add all the remaining ingredients except the pineapple and cashews. Increase the heat to bring to a boil, then reduce the heat to low, cover, and cook for 25–30 minutes, until the sauce has thickened and the lentils are cooked through. Turn off the heat. Stir in the pineapple, cover, and let stand a couple of minutes for the pineapple to warm through. Taste and adjust the seasoning as desired. Serve topped with crushed cashews.

Serving Suggestion: Serve over short-grain brown rice, topped with chopped avocado (tossed in a little lemon juice and sprinkled with salt). Leftovers are wonderful in a salad bowl or wrap!

Italian Ratatouille

Artichokes are spectacular in this ratatouille. I use frozen artichokes; if you're using jarred, drain and rinse them well. The ingredients don't need to simmer for long to yield outstanding flavor!

Serves 4

¼ cup dry red wine *or* water and/ or juice

2 cups chopped sweet or regular onion

1 teaspoon salt

½ teaspoon fennel seed

Freshly ground black pepper to taste

3 cups chopped zucchini

3 cups chopped bell peppers

2 cups chopped artichokes

4–6 medium-large cloves garlic, minced

3 cups chopped fresh tomatoes (I like Roma tomatoes)

½ cup chopped fresh basil (see note)

2 tablespoons fresh thyme and/or oregano leaves *or* 1½ teaspoons fresh rosemary (see note)

¼ cup tomato paste

1–2 tablespoons olive brine from a jar of olives (optional)

Heat a large pot over medium-high heat. Pour in the wine and add the onion, salt, fennel seed, and pepper. Cook for about 5 minutes, until the onion begins to brown and soften. Add the zucchini, bell peppers, and artichokes and cook for another 3–4 minutes. Finally, add the garlic, tomatoes, herbs, and tomato paste. Stir and bring the mixture to a low boil. Reduce the heat to low, cover the pot, and simmer for 15–20 minutes. Taste and adjust seasonings as desired. If you want to add the olive brine, stir it in.

Herb Note: Fresh herbs are best in this dish—they really bring the flavors to life. However, if you don't have fresh herbs, you can substitute about 2 teaspoons dried basil and about 1 teaspoon dried thyme or oregano.

Serving Suggestions: Serve this ratatouille on its own with crusty bread, some nut cheese, and olives. Or, try serving it on top of pasta or a whole grain. If you enjoy the flavor of the olive brine, you can top the dish with sliced kalamata or green olives.

Prep Tip: If you have a quick chopper or food processor, you might want to employ it to chop the veg.

Spanish Rice

This is my version of a dish my mother made often when I was young. The addition of lentils makes it substantial enough to enjoy as a meal, though it can also be served as a side. It's a simple but flavorful dish filled with homey appeal.

Serves 4–5

2–3 tablespoons plus 4¾–5 cups water, divided

1½ cups diced onion

2 teaspoons dried oregano

1½ teaspoons dried basil

1 teaspoon paprika

1–1¼ teaspoons sea salt, plus more to taste

Freshly ground black pepper to taste

1 cup green or French lentils, rinsed

1 cup brown rice (see note)

1–2 dried bay leaves

1 cup diced red bell pepper

⅓ cup tomato paste

1 tablespoon balsamic vinegar

1 teaspoon pure maple syrup

1 cup fresh or frozen corn kernels

Heat a large pot over medium-high heat. Pour in 2 tablespoons water and add the onion, oregano, basil, paprika, salt, and pepper. Stir, cover, and cook for 5–6 minutes, until the onion starts to soften. If the mixture is sticking, add another tablespoon of water. Add the lentils, rice, bay leaves, and 4¾ cups water. Bring to a boil, cover, reduce the heat to low, and simmer for 30 minutes. Add the bell pepper, tomato paste, vinegar, and maple syrup. Cover and cook for 5 minutes, or until the lentils are fully cooked. If they are still firm, add the remaining ¼ cup water and let cook for another few minutes until fully softened. Stir in the corn kernels, cover, and let heat through for a few minutes. Taste and season with additional salt or pepper as desired. Remove the bay leaves and serve.

Rice Note: Since I batch-cook rice, I sometimes have it on hand when making this dish. If you want to use up cooked rice for this dish, use about 2½–3 cups precooked brown rice. When preparing the recipe, reduce the water to 3–3¼ cups, and add the cooked rice along with the bell pepper.

Recipe Renewal!

- Steam kale or spinach and fill a serving bowl. Top with reheated No Butter No Chicken (page 191) and a generous drizzle of Cashew Cream (page 115) or nondairy sour cream.
- Layer between two tortillas and pan-fry as you would a quesadilla. To help the mixture hold to the tortillas, you can spread on a little nut cheese or mash just a little of the No Butter No Chicken mixture. Just don't overfill and it should hold together okay. Once crispy, cut into squares and serve with mango chutney and a plain nondairy yogurt for dipping.

No Butter No Chicken

The popular Indian dish gets a Kind Kitchen makeover with chickpeas, potatoes, and an abundantly flavorful sauce. I most often make this dish with the coconut milk because it is quick and convenient, but the cashew cream is especially luscious, so use it if you can!

Serves 5–6

2–3 tablespoons coconut water or water

2 cups chopped onion

1 tablespoon garam masala

1 teaspoon cumin seed

1 teaspoon ground coriander

½ teaspoon ground cinnamon

¼ teaspoon crushed red pepper

1–1¼ teaspoons salt

Freshly ground black pepper to taste

3 medium-large cloves garlic, minced

1 (28-ounce) can crushed tomatoes

2 (15-ounce) cans chickpeas, rinsed and drained

5 cups cubed red or yellow potato (about 2 pounds; see note)

¼ cup water

1 tablespoon grated fresh ginger (see note)

½–¾ cup Cashew Cream (page 115) or refrigerated canned coconut cream (see note), divided

⅓–½ cup chopped cilantro (optional)

Lemon or lime wedges, for serving

Pour 2 tablespoons coconut water into a large pot and add the onion, spices, salt, and pepper. Sauté over medium-high heat, stirring occasionally, for 6–7 minutes, until the onion has softened. Add another tablespoon of coconut water if the mixture is sticking. Add the garlic and stir for a minute. Add the tomatoes, chickpeas, potatoes, and water. Increase the heat to high and bring the mixture to a boil. Reduce the heat to low, cover, and simmer for 20–30 minutes, until the potatoes are fork-tender. Add the ginger and cream and stir. Add the cilantro (if using) and stir until just wilted. Taste and add more salt and pepper if desired. Serve with lemon wedges.

Potato Note: Waxy red or yellow potatoes will hold their shape best after cooking. (If you use russet potatoes, they will likely break down more in the sauce.)

Ginger Note: I like adding the ginger at the end of cooking to keep it vibrant. You can add it earlier while sautéing the spices, if you prefer, or divide the ginger between the sauce and finishing.

Coconut Cream Note: Use regular (not light) coconut milk in this recipe. Before using, refrigerate the can overnight or for a few days. The thick cream will rise to the top and be easy to scoop and measure. You can use a few tablespoons of the milk portion instead of coconut water to sauté, then add the thick cream to finish.

Pressure Cooker Method: To cook in a multifunction pressure cooker (such as an Instant Pot), follow the instructions to sauté the onion and spices. Add the garlic, tomatoes, chickpeas, and potatoes, omitting the ¼ cup water. Secure the lid and set the valve to the "sealed" position. Press the Manual button and set the cook time for 9 minutes at high pressure. Allow the pot to come to pressure and cook. Once the timer goes off, turn off the pot to allow the pressure to naturally release. Stir in the ginger, cream, and cilantro and season to taste.

Serving Suggestions: Serve over cooked brown rice or another cooked grain, with roti or other flatbreads, along with a sweet chutney.

Stuffed Sweet Potatoes

Simple sweet potatoes get a Southwestern twist with black beans and salsa—and take their rightful place as a main on your plate!

Serves 4

3 pounds sweet potatoes, well scrubbed (see note)

1 cup cooked or canned (rinsed and drained) black beans

½ cup fresh, canned, or frozen corn kernels

½ cup cooked rice or quinoa or more beans

½ cup diced bell pepper

⅓–½ cup sliced green onions

1 cup prepared salsa (see note)

2 teaspoons fresh lime juice

¼ teaspoon sea salt (optional)

1 batch Cashew Cream (page 115), What-amole (page 104), or Sassy Sour Cream (page 103), for topping

¼ cup minced fresh cilantro (optional)

Optional toppings (see note)

Preheat the oven to 425°F. Line a rimmed baking sheet with parchment paper.

Place the whole sweet potatoes (do not pierce) on the prepared baking sheet. Bake for 45–60 minutes, until tender.

While the sweet spuds are baking, combine the beans, corn, grain, bell pepper, green onions, salsa, and lime juice in a large bowl. Toss to combine and set aside.

Remove the cooked potatoes from the oven and keep the oven on. Let the potatoes cool for 10 minutes or more, until they're cool enough to handle. With a sharp knife, slice the top of each sweet potato down its length to open them up into boat shapes. Use an ice cream scoop or spoon to scoop out a little flesh from each—just enough to create a hollow for the topping.

Chop or roughly break up the scooped potato flesh and add it to the bean and salsa mixture. Stir to combine. Top the warm potato shells with the bean and salsa mixture. Return to the oven for 8–10 minutes to heat the toppings. To serve, top each potato with your choice of topping and cilantro (if using).

Sweet Potato Note: Your choice to use orange sweet potatoes, yellow, or even purple! Also, feel free to swap regular potatoes for sweet. If you baked them in advance and they have been refrigerated, reheat in a 400°F oven for about 10 minutes while you prep the topping.

Salsa Note: Consider how much heat you want in these stuffed potatoes and choose a salsa that will suit. The intensity of the salsa will be toned down slightly with the vegetables and beans mixed in. If you are unsure, you can always top off portions of the finished spuds with hot sauce or extra salsa, rather than adding the heat directly to the filling.

Salt Note: Salsa brands can vary significantly in how salty they taste. Freshly prepared salsas are usually less salty than jarred salsa, and jarred salsa brands differ as well. You may want to omit the salt initially, taste the mixture once prepped, and adjust the salt to taste.

Topping Ideas: Other toppings to try include sliced black olives, sliced fresh or jarred hot peppers, vegan cheese or cheese sauce, or chopped avocado.

Fiesta Taco Filling

Tacos are one of the easiest dishes to make vegan, and even easier to make with whole foods you have at home! This filling tastes better and fresher than store-bought vegan taco meats and with more nourishing ingredients.

Serves 4–5

- ½ cup raw sunflower seeds (see note)
- ½ cup raw pumpkin seeds (see note)
- 2 (14-ounce) cans black beans, rinsed and drained
- 2 tablespoons water, plus more as needed
- ¾–1 cup sliced green onions *or* ½ cup diced onion
- ½ cup diced red or green bell pepper
- 2 teaspoons chili powder
- 2 teaspoons dried oregano
- 1½ teaspoons ground cumin
- ½ teaspoon garlic powder
- ½ teaspoon sea salt
- ¼ teaspoon ground cinnamon
- 2 tablespoons tomato paste
- 1 tablespoon fresh lime juice
- 1½ teaspoons tamari

Put the sunflower seeds in a mini-processor or blender and process until crumbly. Add the pumpkin seeds and process again until crumbly (it doesn't have to be very fine). Break up the beans with your fingers, mashing them slightly. (You can also add them to the processor and pulse, but it's easier to just squish the beans with your fingers to break them up.)

Heat a nonstick pan over medium-high heat. Pour in the water and add the onion, bell pepper, chili powder, oregano, cumin, garlic powder, salt, and cinnamon. Cook for 7–8 minutes, stirring occasionally, until the onion has softened. Add extra water if the mixture is sticking. Reduce the heat to medium-low. Add the tomato paste, lime juice, tamari, seed blend, and beans. Stir and cook for another 4–5 minutes to warm the mixture through. The mixture will dry some while warming, but if it's sticking or burning, add another tablespoon or so of water and reduce the heat if needed. Taste, and add any additional seasonings as desired. Let cool slightly before serving.

Seed Note: Sunflower seeds take longer to break up, so it's helpful to start processing those first, before the pumpkin seeds. If you have roasted seeds on hand rather than raw, you can still use them. Roasted seeds are typically salted, so check the ingredients, and if your seeds have salt, reduce or omit the salt in the taco mix.

Serving Suggestions: Pair with What-amole (page 104) in taco shells, or in a taco bowl with greens dressed with Cilantro Lover's Dressing (page 71).

> **Recipe Renewal!** What to do after Taco Tuesday?
> - Layer a casserole dish with cooked quinoa or rice. Distribute the leftover taco filling on top. If it's scant, add more beans and chopped veggies. Top with crumbled tortilla chips or grated prepared polenta (from a tube). Bake at 375°F or 400°F for 20–25 minutes, until heated and golden.
> - Mix the taco filling into quinoa or rice with avocado in a wrap.

8
Holiday Fare

Every holiday season I'm asked, "What do you eat instead of turkey?"
Oh, so many things—all tastier, healthier, and kind. I have shared
many festive, feast-worthy recipes in other books, and here I share
a new main dish, my Holiday Dinner Torte. The "main" dish seems
to be the biggest hurdle for people planning for holiday meals.
This torte will beautifully take center stage on your table. Serve
it with Golden Gravy, add my Cornucopia Salad (page 62) and
any other sides you like, and you're set to entertain in style!

Holiday Dinner Torte

This will make a beautiful centerpiece for any holiday dinner, and looks so festive all flecked with cranberries and herbs. Plus, it offers traditional savory flavors that are homey and comforting.

Serves 6–8

1½ cups diced apple (not large chunks)

1 tablespoon fresh lemon juice

¼ cup dry white wine or water

1½ cups diced onion

2 large cloves garlic, roughly chopped

2 teaspoons poultry seasoning (see note)

¾ teaspoon sea salt, divided

Freshly ground black pepper

2 (15-ounce) cans chickpeas, rinsed and drained

3 tablespoons vegan Worcestershire sauce, plus 1–2 tablespoons for topping

1 tablespoon tahini

2½ cups cooked brown rice

¾ cup toasted pumpkin seeds, plus 2 tablespoons for topping

1 cup rolled oats

2–3 tablespoons dried cranberries or sliced fresh cranberries, for topping (optional)

Preheat the oven to 375°F. Prepare a springform pan with a swipe of oil (optional).

In a small bowl, toss the apples with the lemon juice and set aside.

Heat a large skillet over medium heat. Pour in the wine and add the onion, garlic, poultry seasoning, ¼ teaspoon of the salt, and a few grinds of pepper. Cook for 9–10 minutes, stirring occasionally, until the onion has softened and is turning golden. If the mixture is sticking while cooking, add a few teaspoons of water. Use a teaspoon of water to deglaze the skillet after cooking. With a silicone spatula, scrape the contents of the skillet into a food processor.

Add the chickpeas, 3 tablespoons Worcestershire, tahini, and remaining ½ teaspoon salt to the food processor. Puree until fairly smooth, then add the brown rice, pumpkin seeds, and oats and pulse to mix. Scrape down the food processor and process again, just until the mixture reaches a fairly uniform consistency, but it's fine to keep some texture. Don't overprocess or the rice will become sticky. Scrape the bowl again if needed. Remove the blade from the food processor. Add the apple and mix with a spatula.

Transfer the mixture to the prepared springform pan. Use a spatula to smooth out the mixture, lightly pressing down as you spread mixture evenly. Add the additional vegan Worcestershire to the top and spread over the surface. Sprinkle on the additional pumpkin seeds and the optional cranberries. Bake for 30 minutes, or until slightly firm and the top is lightly browned. Remove and let sit for 5–10 minutes. Remove the outer ring from the springform pan and slice the torte to serve.

Poultry Seasoning Note: Poultry seasoning is a blend of dried herbs that can include sage, thyme, rosemary, marjoram, nutmeg, black pepper, and/or celery seed. If you don't have poultry seasoning, try a mix of 1 teaspoon dried marjoram or oregano, ½ teaspoon dried thyme, ½ teaspoon dried rosemary or sage, and a pinch of ground nutmeg.

Serving Suggestion: Serve with Cran-Apple Compote (page 201) and Golden Gravy (page 202).

Cran-Apple Compote

This twist on a holiday favorite tones down the punch of cranberries with the homey comfort of apples. I like to round out the flavors with just a tablespoon of maple syrup. If you prefer to omit it, this cranberry sauce is sweetened just with fruits!

Makes about 1½ cups

1½ cups diced apple (peeling optional)

1 cup fresh or frozen whole cranberries

2 tablespoons finely chopped dates

¼ teaspoon sea salt

⅛ teaspoon ground allspice *or* pinch ground cloves

⅓–½ cup fresh orange juice

½–1 teaspoon grated orange or lemon zest

1 tablespoon pure maple syrup (optional)

In a pot, combine the apple, cranberries, orange juice, dates, salt, and allspice or cloves. Partially cover the pot and bring the mixture to a boil over medium-high heat, then uncover, reduce the heat to medium-low, and simmer for 12–15 minutes, stirring occasionally. Reduce the heat to low if the sauce is sticking or bubbling too rapidly. Once the cranberries have broken down and the sauce has thickened, stir in the zest and remove from the heat; the sauce will continue to thicken as it cools. Taste, and if you'd like a touch of maple syrup, stir it in.

Golden Gravy

We often wait until the holidays to make gravy. This recipe is so quick and simple, however, you can make it any day of the week.

Makes about 2¼ cups

¼ cup whole-grain flour (spelt or whole-wheat pastry flour, or millet flour for gluten-free)

2 cups vegetable broth, divided

2 tablespoons dry white wine (optional)

1½ tablespoons tahini

1 tablespoon dried onion flakes or chopped shallot

2–3 teaspoons chopped fresh thyme *or* rosemary (or combination of both)

½ teaspoon garlic powder *or* 1 small clove garlic, minced

¼ teaspoon poultry seasoning (see note)

3 tablespoons tamari

1 dried bay leaf

Lemon pepper or freshly ground black pepper to taste

In a medium saucepan, combine the flour, about ½ cup of the vegetable broth, the wine (if using), and the tahini. Begin to whisk, and bring the heat up to medium. Whisk until the mixture thickens into a roux. Slowly add the remaining broth and increase the heat slightly. Continue to whisk, adding the remaining ingredients except the bay leaf and pepper. Increase the heat to bring to a boil. Reduce the heat to low, add the bay leaf, and simmer for 10–15 minutes, stirring occasionally. Taste and add extra seasonings as desired. Remove the bay leaf and serve (see note).

Fresh Herb Note: I love the flavor that fresh herbs add to a gravy. If you don't have them, however, you can substitute dried when adding the garlic powder and poultry seasoning. Use about ½ teaspoon each of dried thyme and rosemary.

Poultry Seasoning Note: Poultry seasoning is a blend of dried herbs that can include sage, thyme, rosemary, marjoram, nutmeg, black pepper, and/or celery seed. If you don't have poultry seasoning, try a couple pinches each of dried rosemary, dried thyme, and dried oregano.

Prep Tip: You can prepare this gravy a couple of days in advance, store in an airtight container in the refrigerator, and gently reheat to serve.

Lemon-Dijon Roasted Potatoes

Though mashed potatoes are traditional holiday fare, I prefer mine roasted. Here, they are infused with a lemon-Dijon marinade highlighted with rosemary. Although they're special enough for a holiday, they are delicious any time of year!

Serves 4–5

2 teaspoons chopped fresh rosemary, thyme, or oregano

½ teaspoon garlic powder (optional)

¼ teaspoon (rounded) sea salt, plus more to taste

Freshly ground black pepper to taste

2 tablespoons fresh lemon juice

1½–2 tablespoons refrigerated canned coconut cream (see note)

2 teaspoons Dijon mustard

2 teaspoons pure maple syrup

3 pounds cubed (about 2 inches) red and/or Yukon Gold potatoes (see note)

Preheat the oven to 400°F. Line a large rimmed baking sheet with parchment paper and wipe the surface of the parchment with just a drop of oil (see note).

In a large bowl, whisk together the rosemary, garlic powder (if using), salt, pepper, lemon juice, coconut cream, mustard, and maple syrup. Add the potatoes and toss to coat. Spread the potatoes in a single layer on the prepared baking sheet, reserving the remaining marinade in the bowl. Bake the potatoes for 30–40 minutes, then drizzle on the remaining marinade and toss. Bake for another 25–30 minutes, until the potatoes have softened and caramelized in spots. Taste and season with extra salt if desired.

Coconut Cream Note: Use regular (not light) coconut milk in this recipe. Before using, refrigerate the can overnight or for a few days. The thick cream will rise to the top and be easy to scoop and measure. Use only the thick cream (reserve the thin coconut milk for another use).

Spud Note: For the holidays, I like to make these straight up with red or Yukon Gold potatoes, since I also serve the Roasted Squash and Sweet Potato Puree (page 206). However, feel free to sub in some yellow, orange, or purple sweet potatoes for some of the white spuds.

Parchment/Oil Note: Some lesser-quality brands of parchment will stick to veggies, oddly. Just a drop of oil, wiped around the paper, prevents sticking. If you have good-quality parchment, the oil can be omitted.

Roasted Squash and Sweet Potato Puree

This puree, or a version of it, shows up at our holiday dinner table every year. I like to combine sweet potatoes with dark winter squash for best flavor. You can use either one in full or any combination you like. It's so good you will want to make it again beyond the holidays!

Serves 4–6

3½–4 pounds mixed dark orange squash and orange sweet potato (see note)

½–¾ teaspoon sea salt

½ teaspoon ground cinnamon

⅛ teaspoon ground nutmeg

⅛ teaspoon ground cardamom (optional)

Freshly ground black pepper to taste

¼ cup plain nondairy milk or canned coconut milk

Preheat the oven to 425°F. Line a rimmed baking sheet with parchment paper.

Pierce the squash a few times with a fork and place on the prepared baking sheet, along with the sweet potatoes. Bake for 50–60 minutes, until very tender when pierced (baking time will vary based on the size of the squash and sweet potatoes). Remove from the oven and set aside until cool enough to handle.

Cut open the squash and sweet potatoes and scoop the flesh from the peels (discard the peels, as well as the seeds and strings from the squash). Place the flesh in a food processor, along with the seasonings (starting with ½ teaspoon salt) and milk. (Alternatively, you can put everything in a large bowl and use a hand blender.) Puree until smooth. Season with additional salt and pepper if desired. Serve immediately or return to the oven on low heat to keep warm.

Squash Note: I like red kuri or butternut squash with the sweet potato in this puree. You can also replace some of the sweet potato with some rutabaga or parsnip if you love those roots! If you already have some cooked squash or spuds on hand, you'll need 6–7 cups. It's a flexible recipe, so you can tweak the seasonings as you go.

Serving Suggestion: Outside of the holidays, use this puree much as you would mashed potatoes: Serve as a side, or as a base to top with a lentil or bean dish, or in a warm salad bowl.

Pressure Cooker New Year's Baked Beans

It's tradition to eat legumes on New Year's Day for good luck. We eat beans every day, but I make some version of baked beans at the start of every new year. On the stovetop or in the oven, the bean prep can take hours. Using a pressure cooker, this version is ready in just over a half hour. Bonus: The beans become delectably tender!

Serves 6–8

3 cups dry navy beans or other small bean

2½–3 cups chopped onion

1 tablespoon dried oregano

1 tablespoon garlic powder

2–3 teaspoons curry powder (see note)

1 teaspoon fennel seed

1 teaspoon dried thyme

½ teaspoon ground allspice

¼ teaspoon ground cardamom

Freshly ground black pepper to taste

2 tablespoons balsamic vinegar

1 teaspoon sea salt

1 large or 2 small bay leaves

1½ cups chopped apple (optional)

4 cups water (or more as needed)

¼ cup tomato paste

2 tablespoons tamari

2 tablespoons molasses

1½ teaspoons pure maple syrup (optional; see note)

Soak the beans overnight, or do a quick soak (see the Guide to Cooking Beans, page 258). After soaking, rinse well and drain.

Set a multifunction pressure cooker (such as an Instant Pot) to sauté. Put the onion, dried herbs and spices, pepper, and vinegar in the pot and cook for 5–7 minutes, stirring frequently, until the onion starts to soften. If the mixture is sticking, add a splash of water. Turn off the sauté function and add the soaked beans, salt, bay leaves, apple (if using), 4 cups of water, tomato paste, tamari, and molasses. Stir to mix well.

Secure the lid and set the valve to the "sealed" position. Press the Manual button and set the cook time for 15 minutes at high pressure. Allow the pot to come to pressure and cook. Once the timer goes off, turn off the pot and allow the pressure to naturally release. Open the pot and allow the beans to cool slightly. (Note: The sauce will still be thin at this point.) Taste and adjust the seasonings, adding the maple syrup and more salt and/or pepper if desired. Then, put the lid back on and let the beans sit in the residual heat for a couple of hours if possible. The more the beans sit, the more they absorb the liquid—and thereby the flavors! Shortly before you're ready to eat, set the pot to "keep warm" until the beans are nice and hot.

Curry Powder Note: The curry powder may seem like an unusual addition to these beans. My mom always added a bit of curry powder to her baked beans. She swore it added a little something. I agree! I like the full 3 teaspoons. If you aren't sure, start with 2.

Maple Syrup Note: The chopped apple adds a natural sweetness. If you're adding the apple you may not want the maple syrup. If you are used to canned baked beans (which are quite sweet), you may enjoy this dish with both!

Prep Tip: While these beans are quick to cook, the flavors and texture are best when you can make them in advance and then reheat. Either make them in the morning and allow them to sit in the pot for several hours before reheating, or make them a few days ahead, then reheat on the stovetop or back in the Instant Pot. The 15 minutes of pressure cooking time is a little longer than needed for most bean recipes, but this helps the beans get very soft and absorb more flavor.

Serving Suggestions: Serve over brown rice or quinoa. Or, serve with crusty bread for dunking—in which case, add another ½ cup water for "saucier" beans.

Recipe Renewal! What to do on January 2 (or any other time you have leftover baked beans)?
- Mix them into pasta with a touch of store-bought pasta sauce. (It may sound odd, but my family loves it!)
- Serve over a sweet potato mash with a side salad.
- Freeze for another day!

Guinnessless Sheet Cake

Our daughter needed an Irish dish for a heritage-themed event at school. This traditional Irish fruitcake recipe received some "kind" treatment, as well as removing the beer from the ingredients. The cake is pleasantly spiced and has a moist crumb like gingerbread—so while delicious anytime of the year, it is especially suited for a holiday table!

Makes 1 (8 × 12-inch) sheet cake; serves 8–10

1¼ cups spelt flour

1 cup oat flour

½ cup coconut sugar

½ cup raisins

1½ teaspoons ground cinnamon

1–1½ teaspoons grated lemon zest

1 teaspoon baking powder

1 teaspoon baking soda

½ teaspoon ground nutmeg

¼–½ teaspoon ground ginger

¼ teaspoon sea salt

1 cup vanilla or plain nondairy milk

¾ cup unsweetened applesauce

2 tablespoons macadamia nut butter or almond butter (optional; see note for nut-free)

1 tablespoon blackstrap molasses

1 tablespoon rice vinegar, apple cider vinegar, or fresh lemon juice

1 teaspoon pure vanilla extract

Preheat the oven to 350°F. Lightly wipe an 8 × 12 baking dish with oil and line with parchment paper.

In a large bowl, combine all the dry ingredients, including the raisins and zest.

In a medium bowl, whisk together the milk, applesauce, nut butter, molasses, vinegar, and vanilla.

Add the wet ingredients to the dry and mix until just combined. Transfer to the prepared baking dish. Bake for 26–29 minutes, until a toothpick or skewer inserted in the center of the cake comes out clean. Remove from the oven, and let the cake cool in the pan.

Nut Butter/Nut-Free Note: If using nut butter, use one that is "runny" or loose, rather than a dense, thick nut butter. I have tested this cake without nut butter at all, and it's still beautiful! To make it nut-free, omit the nut butter and increase the applesauce to 1 cup.

Serving Suggestions: Pair with a scoop of vanilla nondairy yogurt, a dollop of Dessert Cashew Cream (page 246), or a drizzle of Coconut-Date Caramel Cream (page 247).

9

Home Sweet Home

The sweet treats here are all made without refined oil, and there's a little something for everyone. Everything inside and out of the cookie jar is here, from cookies and bars to cakes to gelato and sauces—and beyond! You'll find Charming Apple Crisp, Maui Gelato (made with purple sweet potatoes!), Mythical Cheesecake (no nuts!), Heavenly Baklava, Yellow Sweet Potato Cake with Yellow Sweets Frosting, and more. They are all so good, you might not know where to start! If you're looking for inspiration, check out the Honest Chocolate Chip Cookies. I created my Homestyle Chocolate Chip Cookies back in 2004 for *Vive le Vegan!*, and to this day I hear from readers that it's still their favorite chocolate chip cookie. I think this new recipe rivals those homestyle chippers!

Honest Chocolate Chip Cookies

My Homestyle Chocolate Chip Cookies from my 2004 cookbook *Vive le Vegan!* broke vegan cookie ground. They are the beloved chocolate chip cookie recipe in the vegan community. For this book I was determined to create a cookie as good or better—without a refined oil. This is it, my friends. Honestly, it's just as good as the original!

Makes 12–14 cookies

1 cup plus 2–3 tablespoons spelt flour *or* 1 cup white whole-wheat flour or pastry flour

¼ cup unrefined sugar (can substitute coconut sugar, will just be darker)

1 teaspoon baking powder

¼ teaspoon (rounded) baking soda

¼ teaspoon salt

⅓ cup pure maple syrup

3 tablespoons refrigerated canned coconut cream (see note)

2 tablespoons coconut butter, softened (see note)

1½ teaspoons pure vanilla extract

¼ teaspoon molasses

½ cup nondairy chocolate chips

Preheat the oven to 350°F. Line a rimmed baking sheet with parchment paper.

In a mixing bowl, stir together the flour (starting with 1 cup + 2 tbsp), sugar, baking powder, baking soda, and salt until well combined. In another bowl, combine the maple syrup, coconut cream, coconut butter, vanilla, and molasses. Stir to mix.

Add the wet ingredients to the dry, along with the chocolate chips, and stir until well combined. If the mixture seems a little loose, add the remaining 1 tablespoon flour and stir through. Chill the batter in the fridge for 15–20 minutes, if possible.

Scoop small mounds of the batter (about 1½ tablespoons each) onto the prepared baking sheet. Flatten the cookies lightly with your fingers or a spatula. Bake for 12 minutes, or until the cookies are golden around the edges. Remove and let cool for a few minutes on the pan, then transfer to a cooling rack.

Coconut Cream Note: Use regular (not light) coconut milk in this recipe. Before using, refrigerate the can overnight or for a few days. The thick cream will rise to the top and be easy to scoop and measure. Use only the thick cream (reserve the thin coconut milk for another use). For this recipe, remove a little more than 3 tablespoons, so that when it softens/melts it will evenly fill 3 tablespoons. You can warm some of the thick cream in a hot water bath or in the preheating oven if needed.

Coconut Butter Note: In warm months, the coconut butter will be naturally softened. In cooler months, use a butter knife to piece out the firm coconut butter, estimating just a little over 2 tablespoons. Put it in a heatproof bowl or measuring cup and place it in the oven for a few minutes while it preheats. Just don't forget it or it will burn! Remove after a few minutes, stir, and use in the recipe. Or, heat for just 5 seconds in the microwave, stir, and then heat for another 5 seconds.

Recipe Renewal! Who has leftover cookies? Kidding! But, if you want to make something new with these (or other) cookies . . .
- crumble into nondairy ice cream for a chunky ice cream.
- scoop nondairy ice cream between two cookies, press together, and cover in plastic wrap to freeze for ice cream cookie sandwiches!

Recharged! Cookies

My third cookbook, *Eat, Drink, & Be Vegan,* had a recipe for Super-Charge Me! Cookies. They were a hot cookie. My family loved them; readers loved them! I wanted to make a version that was gluten-free (with an oat base) and also without added oil. Now, these cookies are Recharged!

Makes about 12 cookies

1 cup quick oats or rolled oats

1 cup oat flour

¼ cup raisins or chopped dried fruit

¼ cup nondairy chocolate chips

¼ cup unsweetened shredded coconut

½ teaspoon baking powder

½ teaspoon baking soda

¼–½ teaspoon ground cinnamon

¼ teaspoon sea salt

3 tablespoons flax meal (not flax seed)

½ cup pure maple syrup

3 tablespoons almond butter or other nut butter

2–2½ tablespoons coconut butter (see note)

1 tablespoon pure vanilla extract

Preheat the oven to 350°F. Line a rimmed baking sheet with parchment paper.

In a mixing bowl, combine the oats, oat flour, raisins, chocolate chips, coconut, baking powder, baking soda, cinnamon, and salt and stir until well combined. In a separate bowl, combine the flax meal, maple syrup, almond butter, coconut butter, and vanilla. Stir until well combined.

Add the wet mixture to the dry and mix until well combined. Scoop 2–2½ tablespoons of batter (use a cookie scoop if you have one) and place level mounds of the batter on the prepared baking sheet, spacing the cookies. Use your fingers to flatten the cookies (moisten your hands if sticking). Bake for 14 minutes, or until set to the touch and a little golden. Cool on the baking sheet for about a minute, then transfer to a cooling rack.

Coconut Butter Note: For this recipe, I measure the coconut butter at room temperature, not warmed and softened. If it's too hard to mix with the maple syrup and almond butter, you can gently warm the wet mixture (briefly in the oven, or in a hot water bath).

Shmoopy Cookies

These are *really* good. They're a little crunchy and also chewy—sure to perfectly satisfy those cookie cravings for your special shmoopy!

Makes 18–22 cookies

1 cup rolled oats

¾ cup almond flour (see note for nut-free)

½ cup oat flour

½ cup unsweetened shredded coconut

½ cup pumpkin seeds

⅓ cup cocoa powder

¼ cup raisins

3 tablespoons nondairy chocolate chips

1½ teaspoons baking powder

¼ teaspoon sea salt

½ cup pure maple syrup

¼ cup brown rice syrup or coconut nectar

1 teaspoon pure vanilla extract

Preheat the oven to 350°F. Line a rimmed baking sheet with parchment paper.

In a mixing bowl, combine the oats, almond flour, oat flour, coconut, pumpkin seeds, cocoa powder, raisins, chocolate chips, baking powder, and salt. Stir until well combined. In another bowl, stir together the maple syrup, brown rice syrup, and vanilla. Add the wet mixture to the dry and stir until combined.

Scoop mounds of batter (1½ tablespoons each) onto the prepared baking sheet. Bake for 13–15 minutes, until set to the touch. Let the cookies cool on the baking sheet for a minute, then transfer to a cooling rack.

Nut-Free Note: You can also use cashew meal (ground cashews) or, for a nut-free option, try tiger nut flour or ground pumpkin seeds (pumpkin meal).

Nummy Brownie Bites

I'm a little in love with these brownie bites. They are a little crisp on the outside, and soft and moist and dense on the inside, like fudgy brownies.

Makes 13–15 brownie bites

½ cup pitted dates (see note)

⅓ cup pure maple syrup

2 tablespoons almond butter or other nut butter

1½ teaspoons pure vanilla extract

1 cup almond meal

½ cup oat flour

¼ cup cocoa powder

1½ teaspoons baking powder

¼ teaspoon (rounded) sea salt

2 tablespoons nondairy chocolate chips

Preheat the oven to 325°F. Line a rimmed baking sheet with parchment paper.

In the bowl of a stand mixer fitted with the paddle attachment, combine the dates and maple syrup. Process on low speed to incorporate, then increase the speed slightly to fully pulverize and smooth the dates. Since dates can vary by brand, this may take a few minutes or longer. It's okay to see a little texture in the date puree, but no big obvious pieces—it will continue to smooth as you add the other ingredients. Add the nut butter and vanilla and mix again until smooth and the ingredients are incorporated. Add the almond meal, oat flour, cocoa powder, baking powder, and salt. Process on low speed until the ingredients come together into a sticky batter. Stir in the chocolate chips.

Scoop the batter into small mounds (about 1 tablespoon each) onto the prepared baking sheet. Bake for 12–13 minutes, until set to the touch (they will be a little soft in the center). Let the brownie bites cool on the pan for about a minute, then transfer to a cooling rack.

Date Notes: If your dates aren't very soft, soak them in the maple syrup for about 30 minutes.

Mixer Note: If you don't have a stand mixer with a paddle attachment, you can use a small food processor (a hand mixer will not be strong enough). First puree the dates with the maple syrup, then add the almond butter and vanilla and puree. Once the mixture is fairly smooth (it doesn't have to be silky smooth), scrape into a larger bowl. Add all the dry ingredients except the chocolate chips and mix by hand until well incorporated, then stir in the chocolate chips.

Raspberry-Coconut Crumble Bars

This is a reinvented version of a dessert square bar that I had in my first cookbook, *The Everyday Vegan*. I loved them then, and many of you did as well. I had wanted to refresh the recipe for years. Now it's gluten-free and oil-free—and tastes better than ever!

Makes 16 squares

Base

1½ cups oat flour

1 cup unsweetened shredded coconut

½ teaspoon pure vanilla bean powder

¼ teaspoon sea salt

¼ cup coconut nectar

2 tablespoons nondairy milk

2 tablespoons coconut butter, softened (see note)

Filling

1 cup natural raspberry jam (see note)

Topping

¼ cup oat flour

¼ cup unsweetened shredded coconut

2 teaspoons unrefined sugar or coconut sugar

Pinch salt

1 tablespoon nondairy milk

2 teaspoons coconut butter

Preheat the oven to 350°F. Wipe or spray a 9-inch square baking pan with a smidgen of oil, then line the pan with parchment paper, letting the paper overhang the edges of the pan.

In a mixing bowl, combine the ingredients for the base. Use your fingers or a spoon to work the ingredients together. The mixture should hold together when pressed between your fingers. Press the base layer into the prepared baking pan in an even layer.

Spoon the jam on top and spread over the surface of the base.

In a small bowl, combine the topping ingredients, working together with your fingers to get a crumbly texture. Sprinkle the topping over the jam layer.

Bake for 20 minutes. Let cool completely in the pan. When ready to cut, remove the bars from the pan by lifting up the edges of the parchment. Cut into 16 squares.

Coconut Butter Note: In warm months, the coconut butter will be naturally softened. In cooler months, use a butter knife to piece out the firm coconut butter, estimating just a little over 2 tablespoons. Put it in a heatproof bowl or measuring cup and place it in the oven for a few minutes while it preheats. Just don't forget it or it will burn! Remove after a few minutes, stir, and use in the recipe. Or, heat for just 5 seconds in the microwave, stir, and then heat for another 5 seconds.

Jam Note: While you can certainly substitute another berry jam you like, there is a beautiful flavor contrast with the raspberry. It's just slightly tart against the sweet oaty base!

Crackle Blender Brownies

Now that I have your attention, these brownies are made with . . . lentils! Don't turn the page. These are epic! Once you try them, you'll forget I even mentioned it.

Makes 16–20 brownies

1 cup cooked red lentils, cooled (see note)

½ cup cocoa powder

¼ cup coconut sugar

¼ cup arrowroot powder

1 teaspoon baking powder

¼ teaspoon sea salt

½ cup brown rice syrup (see note)

½ cup refrigerated canned coconut cream (see note)

2 tablespoons coconut butter or a thick, dense nut butter

2 teaspoons pure vanilla extract

¼–⅓ cup chocolate chips, divided

optional coarse sea salt for topping

Preheat the oven to 425°F. Spray or wipe a nonstick 8-inch brownie pan with a bit of oil and line with parchment paper, letting the paper overhang the edges of the pan.

In a blender, combine all the ingredients except the chocolate chips. Puree slowly at first to incorporate the ingredients, then increase the blender speed and puree for several seconds until fully smooth.

Sprinkle most of the chocolate chips into the prepared pan before adding the batter, scattering more or less evenly. Pour the batter into the pan. Sprinkle on the remaining chips, and a couple pinches of coarse sea salt, if using. Bake for 12 minutes, then reduce the oven temperature to 350°F and bake for 22 minutes more, or until the brownies look dry and crackly around the edges. Let the brownies cool completely in the pan. If you like, transfer to the refrigerator to cool even more (this will make slicing easier). Remove the brownies from the pan by lifting up the edges of the parchment. Cut into squares.

Lentil Note: Cook and cool the lentils in advance. They should be dense and not watery. Rather than cook a very small amount of dry red lentils for this recipe, it's easiest to cook a larger batch of red lentils, and then portion out the 1 cup to use in this recipe. Extra lentils can be refrigerated for 5–6 days, or frozen for later use in stews, chilis, sauces, hummus, etc. You can also portion 1-cup amounts and freeze to use in this recipe—simply thaw lentils before pureeing.

Brown Rice Syrup Note: Brown rice syrup works best for this recipe. If you don't want to use it or cannot find it, substitute a thick coconut nectar that is close to the texture of brown rice syrup or corn syrup.

Coconut Cream Note: Use regular (not light) coconut milk in this recipe. Before using, refrigerate the can overnight or for a few days. The thick cream will rise to the top and be easy to scoop and measure. Use only the thick cream (reserve the thin coconut milk for another use).

Dreena's Nanaimo Bars

Originating out of Nanaimo, British Columbia, this traditional Canadian no-bake dessert bar has a crumb base, a creamy middle layer, and chocolate ganache on top. Conventional versions use a great deal of white sugar, along with butter and eggs. This Kind Kitchen version is gluten-free and nut-free, and no vegan margarine is needed! (Not "health food" exactly, but quite an improvement on the original—and readers tell me they taste better!)

Makes 16–20 bars

Base

1½ cups pitted dates

½ cup rolled oats

¼ cup cocoa powder

¼ teaspoon salt

½ teaspoon pure vanilla extract

¼ cup raw pumpkin seeds or almond meal

¼ cup unsweetened shredded coconut

Middle

¾–1 cup natural icing sugar (see note)

¼ teaspoon ground turmeric (optional)

⅛ teaspoon sea salt

¾ cup coconut butter

3 tablespoons vanilla nondairy milk *or* full-fat canned coconut milk (see note)

½ teaspoon pure vanilla extract *or* ¼ teaspoon pure vanilla bean powder

Topping

1 cup chopped nondairy chocolate bar or chocolate chips

2½ tablespoons full-fat canned coconut milk or other nondairy milk (see note)

Line an 8-inch square baking pan with parchment paper.

To prepare the base, put the dates and oats in a food processor and pulse several times, until they start to come together and get slightly crumbly. Add the cocoa powder, salt, and vanilla and process until the mixture starts to become sticky. Add the pumpkin seeds and coconut and process until the mixture is very sticky and holds together when pressed with your fingers. Press the mixture into the prepared baking pan. Chill in the refrigerator while you proceed with the next layers.

Add all the ingredients for the middle layer including the turmeric (if using) to a mini processor (see note) and pulse until just combined and smooth. Try not to overblend, as the mixture will heat and become oily. Transfer to the baking pan, spreading the mixture evenly over the base layer. Place the pan back in the refrigerator.

Prepare a hot water bath to make the topping: Fill a small saucepan with several inches of water and heat it over low heat. Put a heatproof bowl on top of the saucepan to hover over the simmering water (be sure it fully covers the top of the saucepan to prevent steam from entering the bowl). Put the chocolate and coconut milk in the bowl and heat gently, stirring occasionally, until the chips are totally melted and the mixture is smooth. Pour the chocolate topping over the top of your bars, and refrigerate until set. To serve, cut into 16–20 bars. Leftover bars can be frozen, if they last that long!

Icing Sugar Note: Natural icing sugars are blended from unrefined cane sugar and are less processed than standard icing sugar. If you don't have a ready-made natural icing sugar, you can pulse coconut sugar in the blender until it's very fine; it will give the filling a natural caramel color rather than the traditional yellow. Using the full 1 cup sugar makes a thicker, slightly firmer center layer. My recipe testers and I agreed that the ¾ cup version was sweet enough for us!

Milk Note: I really enjoy the subtle flavor of a vegan eggnog at the holidays, using either almond, soy, or coconut nog.

Food Processor Note: My food processor has a 16-cup capacity, so I break out my mini processor to make the middle layer; it's hard to get the right consistency in a big processor. If you used a smaller food processor to make the base, you can use the same one to make the middle layer; just clean it out in between.

Yellow Sweet Potato Cake

With the wild popularity of my Chocolate Sweet Potato Cake from *Plant-Powered Families*, I had to re-create it in another flavor. This vanilla version is just as good—maybe better! The yellow sweet potato adds mellow sweetness, moisture, and a tender crumb. Frosted with my dreamy Yellow Sweets Frosting (page 230), it's a spectacular special occasion cake.

Makes 2 (9-inch) cake layers; serves 8

1 cup cooked yellow sweet potato flesh, cooled (see note)

3 tablespoons raw cashew pieces *or* 2 tablespoons hemp seeds

1½ cups nondairy milk

2 teaspoons pure vanilla extract

1½ teaspoons fresh lemon juice

2 cups spelt flour *or* 2 cups less 2 tablespoons white whole-wheat flour

½ cup plus 2 tablespoons unrefined sugar (see note)

2 teaspoons baking powder

¼ teaspoon baking soda

¼ teaspoon sea salt

Preheat the oven to 350°F. Lightly wipe two 9-inch round cake pans with just a smidgen of coconut or other oil, then fit a round of parchment paper on the bottom of each pan.

Combine the sweet potato, cashews, milk, vanilla, and lemon juice in a blender (or in a deep cup if using an immersion blender) and puree until completely smooth.

In a large bowl, combine the flour, sugar, baking powder, baking soda, and salt.

Add the wet ingredients to the dry (be sure to scrape out all the blended ingredients with a silicone spatula). Mix until well incorporated. Transfer to the prepared pans. Bake for 21–23 minutes, until the batter looks dry in the center and is set to the touch. Transfer to a wire rack to cool completely in the pans. Carefully invert the pans to remove the cakes, and frost as desired.

Sweet Potato Note: I use yellow sweet potato in this recipe for a light-colored cake. You can certainly substitute orange sweet potato for the yellow.

Sugar Note: While I normally use coconut sugar as a dry sweetener in recipes, here a lighter sugar is optimal for color. Feel free to use coconut sugar, or even date sugar, if you prefer.

Yellow Sweets Frosting

When blended with coconut butter and a few other ingredients, cooked yellow sweet potatoes transform into a thick, creamy, and not-too-sweet frosting. It's perfect on my Yellow Sweet Potato Cake (page 229), or even on its own, if that's how you roll—I get it!

Makes about 4 cups

2 cups cooked yellow sweet potato flesh, cooled (see note)

¾ cup unrefined sugar, plus more as needed (see note)

½ teaspoon sea salt

About 1 cup coconut butter, not melted (see note)

⅔ cup vanilla or plain nondairy milk, plus more as needed

½ teaspoon (rounded) pure vanilla bean powder (optional)

Combine the sweet potato, sugar, salt, coconut butter (starting with ½ cup; see note), and milk in a high-speed blender (see note). Process until very smooth, scraping down the blender as needed. If it's not blending well, add another 2–3 tablespoons milk to assist the pureeing. Taste and add 1–2 more tablespoons sugar if desired. Add the vanilla bean powder (if using) and stir with a spatula. Transfer to a container and refrigerate until ready to use. Or, get a spoon and dig in!

Sweet Potato Note: You can cook the sweet potatoes in any way that's convenient, though I find the flavor and texture is best with roasting the potatoes whole. See page 11 for tips on roasting.

Coconut Butter Note: The amount of coconut butter depends on the strength of your blender. If you start with a full cup, it can be too sticky for the machine to puree. So begin with ½ cup, then add ⅓ cup, and then the rest if the pureeing is going well. A full cup will give a frosting that sets a little better.

Sugar Note: While coconut sugar or date sugar may be preferable from a whole-foods perspective, an unrefined cane sugar works best for color in this recipe. When it's a special occasion, just go for it!

Blender Note: A high-speed blender makes a world of difference with recipes like this. If you don't have one, try pureeing the coconut butter with the sweet potato in a food processor to begin, then transfer to a blender to fully blend.

Mango Carrot Cake

This cake tastes like a classic carrot cake, and the pureed mango adds fruity sweetness and moisture without the use of oil. Perfect to pair with tea and company.

Makes 1 (8-inch) square cake; serves 6–8

Cake

1½ cups spelt flour

½ cup almond meal

3 tablespoons coconut sugar

1 teaspoon ground cinnamon

¼ teaspoon sea salt

¼ teaspoon ground allspice

¼ teaspoon ground nutmeg

1½ teaspoons baking powder

½ teaspoon baking soda

1 cup frozen mango chunks (see note)

½ cup mashed overripe banana

½ cup pure maple syrup

¼ cup plain nondairy milk

1 teaspoon fresh lemon juice or apple cider vinegar

1 teaspoon pure vanilla extract

1 cup grated carrots

Frosting

⅓ cup coconut butter, softened (see note)

⅛ teaspoon sea salt

3–3½ tablespoons nondairy milk

3–3½ tablespoons pure maple syrup

2 teaspoons fresh lemon juice

Topping (optional)

Chopped pumpkin seeds

Preheat the oven to 350°F. Wipe an 8-inch square glass baking pan with a light coat of oil, then line the pan with parchment paper.

In a large bowl, combine the flour, almond meal, coconut sugar, cinnamon, salt, allspice, and nutmeg; sift in the baking powder and baking soda.

In a blender, combine the mango, banana, maple syrup, milk, lemon juice, and vanilla. Puree until smooth.

Add the wet mixture to the dry, along with the carrots. Stir until well combined. Pour the mixture into the prepared pan. Bake for 35–40 minutes, until a toothpick or skewer inserted in the center comes out clean. Transfer to a wire rack to cool completely in the pan.

To make the frosting, gently warm the coconut butter either by placing the jar in a hot water bath or by placing the measured ⅓ cup in a warm oven (about 250°F) until it softens. Put the coconut butter in a bowl and add all the other frosting ingredients (starting with 3 tablespoons each milk and maple syrup). Stir until well combined. Add extra milk and/or syrup as needed to thin and sweeten as desired.

Use a spatula to spread the frosting over the cooled cake and sprinkle with chopped pumpkin seeds if desired. Chill and serve!

Mango Note: I have tested this cake with frozen pineapple and it is also delicious! Because pineapple is sweeter, use a scant ½ cup maple syrup.

Coconut Butter Note: If you don't want to use coconut butter, substitute raw cashew butter. You won't need as much milk to thin, since it isn't as dry as coconut butter. Start with 1 tablespoon milk, then adjust as needed.

Make Muffins: You can make this batter into muffins if you prefer. Fill 11–12 lined cups and bake for 23–25 minutes.

Date-Sweetened Bundt Cake with Lemon-Maple Glaze

This delicious Bundt cake is sweetened with dates and drizzled with a tart-sweet lemon-maple frosting!

Makes 1 cake; serves about 10–12

Cake

2 cups lightly packed pitted dates (about 10 ounces)

1¾ cups water

½ cup refrigerated canned coconut cream (see note)

¼ cup plain or vanilla nondairy milk

¼ cup pure maple syrup

2 teaspoons pure vanilla extract

1 cup whole-wheat pastry flour

1 cup oat flour

2 teaspoons baking powder

½ teaspoon baking soda

½–1 teaspoon grated lemon zest

½ teaspoon ground cinnamon

½ teaspoon (scant) salt

Lemon-Maple Glaze

2 tablespoons coconut butter, softened, or cashew butter

2–2½ tablespoons pure maple syrup

1 tablespoon fresh lemon juice

Pinch salt

¼ teaspoon grated lemon zest (optional)

Preheat the oven to 350°F. Lightly wipe or spray a Bundt pan with oil (if you have a very good nonstick Bundt pan, you may not need this), then evenly dust the pan with flour. Tap the pan to distribute the flour.

Put the dates and water in a large saucepan. Bring to a boil, then reduce the heat to medium-low and simmer for 5–7 minutes to soften the dates. Remove from the heat. Add the coconut cream, milk, maple syrup, and vanilla and use an immersion blender to puree (alternatively, wait for the mixture to cool and transfer to a blender to puree). Cool for about 15 minutes.

In a mixing bowl, combine the flours, baking powder, baking soda, zest, cinnamon, and salt, stirring well. Add the date mixture to the dry ingredients. Stir until fully combined.

Transfer the batter to the prepared pan, using a spatula to scrape out all the mixture. Tip the pan back and forth a little to even out the level of batter. Bake for 38–40 minutes, until a toothpick inserted in the center comes out clean, or the cake springs back when lightly pressed. Transfer the cake to a wire rack to cool for 15 minutes in the pan. Invert to remove the cake and cool completely on the rack.

While the cake is cooling, prepare the glaze. In a small bowl, stir together the coconut butter, maple syrup, lemon juice, and salt. Stir until smooth. If it's difficult to mix, warm a little in a bowl in a hot water bath or in a warm oven. Spoon the glaze over the cooled cake and use a spatula to swirl more evenly. Sprinkle on the lemon zest, if using. Let the glaze cool.

Coconut Cream Note: Use regular (not light) coconut milk in this recipe. Before using, refrigerate the can overnight or for a few days. The thick cream will rise to the top and be easy to scoop and measure. Use only the thick cream (reserve the thin coconut milk for another use).

Mythical Cheesecake

This is like the unicorn of vegan cheesecakes. Without dairy, most cheesecakes are made either with processed vegan cream cheese substitutes or with nuts like cashews. This one has neither! The magic happens when yellow sweet potato combines with coconut, lemon juice, and a few other key ingredients into an unbelievably luscious filling.

Makes 1 cheesecake; serves 8

Crust

1¼ cups rolled oats

1 cup pitted dates

½ cup pumpkin seeds

⅛ teaspoon sea salt

1 teaspoon pure vanilla extract

Filling

1 cup plus 1–2 tablespoons coconut butter (see note)

¾ cup cooked yellow sweet potato flesh, cooled (see note)

½ cup plain or vanilla nondairy yogurt

⅓ cup refrigerated canned coconut cream (see note)

⅓ cup pure maple syrup

¼ cup fresh lemon juice

¼ teaspoon (scant) sea salt

½ teaspoon pure vanilla bean powder *or* 1 teaspoon pure vanilla extract (optional)

½–1 teaspoon grated lemon zest

Line a 9-inch springform pan or 9–10-inch pie plate with parchment paper.

To prepare the crust, combine the oats, dates, pumpkin seeds, salt, and vanilla in a food processor. Pulse to begin to incorporate the ingredients, then process until the mixture becomes sticky and begins to form a dough on the blade. It will take time to break down the components; give it about 2 minutes and see the magic happen! The heat from the processing will break down the fat in the pumpkin seeds and the mixture will come together. Transfer the mixture to the prepared pan, pressing the mixture onto the base (and up the sides, if you like, but I prefer the crust at the bottom only).

Combine all the ingredients for the filling (except the lemon zest) in a blender (preferably a high-powered blender). Puree until very, very smooth, stopping to scrape down the blender a couple of times as needed. Add the lemon zest and stir in with a spatula. Pour the mixture on top of the crust and spread with a spatula to distribute. Cover the pan with aluminum foil and refrigerate to set overnight, or at least 3 hours.

Coconut Butter Note: If your coconut butter is very hard and difficult to spoon out to measure, you may want to place the jar in a warm water bath for 20 minutes or so. If the coconut butter is cooperative for measuring, you can generously fill the cup and eyeball the measurement rather than measuring the extra 1–2 tablespoons.

Sweet Potato Note: Yellow sweet potato works so beautifully in this recipe. It adds body, a touch of sweetness, and a hint of color. If you want to use orange sweet potato, the color will change quite a lot—and the potato flavor will be more noticeable. If you do use it, I recommend making an orange cheesecake, replacing the lemon zest with orange zest and replacing the vanilla with 1 teaspoon pure orange extract.

Coconut Cream Note: Use regular (not light) coconut milk in this recipe. Before using, refrigerate the can overnight or for a few days. The thick cream will rise to the top and be easy to scoop and measure. Use only the thick cream (reserve the thin coconut milk for another use).

Serving Suggestion: Serve topped with Strawberry Sauce Forever, page 248.

Charming Apple Crisp

I guarantee this will become a favorite dessert for you. My testers raved about it, and my own family was sad when I was finished with my testing for it. It's better than any butter or oil-based crisp—and even better than apple pie!

Serves 4–5

Crisp Topping

¼ cup coconut butter, softened

1½ tablespoons pure maple syrup

1 cup rolled oats

¼ cup coconut sugar

3 tablespoons oat flour

⅛ teaspoon sea salt

Fruit Mixture

¼ cup pure maple syrup

1 tablespoon arrowroot powder or organic cornstarch

1 teaspoon ground cinnamon

⅛ teaspoon ground nutmeg

⅛ teaspoon sea salt

1½ tablespoons fresh lemon juice

1 tablespoon water

5 cups peeled, cored, and thinly sliced apples

3–4 tablespoons raisins or dried cranberries (optional)

1½ tablespoons coconut sugar

Preheat the oven to 350°F. Have ready a 9-inch glass baking dish.

For the topping, in a mixing bowl, combine the coconut butter and maple syrup and stir well. Add the oats, coconut sugar, oat flour, and salt and mix until crumbly.

For the fruit mixture, in a large bowl, whisk together the maple syrup and arrowroot. Add the cinnamon, nutmeg, salt, water, and lemon juice and whisk again. Stir in the sliced apples and raisins, if using, and toss to coat.

Sprinkle the coconut sugar in the bottom of the baking dish. Distribute the apple filling in the baking dish, pouring the juices over the top. Add the crisp topping, distributing it evenly over the apples. Bake for 30–35 minutes, until the apples are soft, using a sharp knife to pierce through the apples to test for doneness at 30 minutes. Remove from the oven and let cool a little before serving.

Serving Suggestions: Serve topped with Dessert Cashew Cream (page 246), vanilla nondairy yogurt, or vanilla nondairy ice cream.

Heavenly Baklava

One of my all-time favorite treats, baklava is crunchy, sweet, and sticky phyllo layered with a cinnamon-infused nut mixture that always hits the sweet spot! This version is big on flavor without the need for added oil or margarine. (While commercial phyllo dough does contain oil, it's a very small amount.) This dessert can be a special occasion treat to impress guests, especially at parties and holidays.

Serves 8 or more

Nut Mixture
¾ cup almonds (see note)

¾ cup pecans (see note)

3 tablespoons coconut sugar

1½ teaspoons ground cinnamon

½ teaspoon grated lemon zest

¼ teaspoon pure vanilla bean powder (optional)

¼ teaspoon sea salt

Phyllo Layers
4–6 tablespoons refrigerated canned coconut cream (see note)

¼ cup almond meal

2 tablespoons coconut sugar

½ (1-pound) package frozen phyllo pastry dough, thawed

Syrup
½ cup plus 2 tablespoons agave nectar or coconut nectar

1½–2 tablespoons fresh lemon juice

Preheat the oven to 350°F. Have ready an 8 × 11-inch baking dish.

Put the almonds in a food processor and process until crumbly. Add the pecans and process until you have a fine nut meal. Add the remaining ingredients for the nut mixture and pulse.

Wipe the inside of the baking dish with a dab of coconut cream. Cut the phyllo dough to roughly fit the bottom of the dish (the sheets should fit into the bottom of the dish and not drape up the sides).

In a small bowl, combine the almond meal and sugar (to sprinkle between the phyllo layers).

Begin to layer your phyllo sheets. Very lightly brush each of the first 2 sheets with coconut cream and sprinkle with about 1 teaspoon of the almond meal mix. Layer on the third sheet and add ¼–⅓ cup of the pureed nut mixture. Layer with another 3 sheets of phyllo, again brushing the first 2 sheets with a touch of coconut cream and sprinkling with the almond meal mix, then adding the nut mixture after the third sheet. Continue this layering until all the nut mixture is used. (You will get 5 or 6 layers total.) For the top layer, use a more generous amount of the coconut cream and a dusting of the almond meal mixture.

Before baking, score the baklava in a diamond pattern or squares with a sharp knife, cutting into the baklava almost through to the bottom. Bake for 35–45 minutes, until golden. Remove from the oven and let cool.

When the baklava is mostly cooled, combine the nectar and lemon juice in a small saucepan. Allow the syrup to come to a slow bubble over medium-low heat. Once bubbling, remove the syrup from the heat and slowly drizzle it over the cooled baklava. Try to distribute it fairly evenly rather than pouring it all in one area. Allow the baklava to cool enough to cut into pieces along the score lines.

Nut Note: For this recipe, the exact amount of each nut doesn't really matter; you want a total of 1½ cups of almonds and pecans, kept separate for processing; almonds are much harder than pecans, so it's helpful to process them first, and then add the pecans once the almonds have become mealy.

Coconut Cream Note: Use regular (not light) coconut milk in this recipe. Before using, refrigerate the can overnight or for a few days. The thick cream will rise to the top and be easy to scoop and measure. Use only the thick cream (reserve the thin coconut milk for another use).

Vanilla Custards

The idea of creating a sweet yet simple vanilla custard played in my mind for years. I don't know why I held back! These are magnificent—velvety textured cream with pure vanilla bean powder. Quite divine (and easy to make)!

Serves 5–6

1 cup raw cashews (not soaked)

⅓ cup unrefined sugar (see note)

¼ teaspoon pure vanilla bean powder (see note)

¼ teaspoon salt

1 cup vanilla or plain nondairy milk

½ cup refrigerated canned coconut cream (see note)

Preheat the oven to 375°F. Place 5 or 6 ramekins (see note) in a 13 × 9-inch baking dish. Fill a kettle with water and bring it to a boil.

While the water comes to a boil, combine all the ingredients in a blender. Puree until very smooth, with no cashew pieces remaining. Pour the pureed mixture into the ramekins.

Slide out the middle oven rack and place the baking dish on the rack. Pour boiling water into the baking dish, filling about halfway up the sides of the ramekins, and being careful not to spill water into the ramekins. Carefully slide the rack back into the oven. Bake for 25–27 minutes (25 minutes for 6 ramekins, 27 for 5), until the custards are set around the edges but still a touch loose in the center. Carefully remove the baking dish from the oven. Remove the ramekins from the water bath and transfer to a cooling rack. Let the custards cool to your desired temperature; they can be served warm, but they can also be refrigerated and served later, chilled.

Coconut Cream Note: Use regular (not light) coconut milk in this recipe. Before using, refrigerate the can overnight or for a few days. The thick cream will rise to the top and be easy to scoop and measure. Use only the thick cream (reserve the thin coconut milk for another use).

Sugar Note: While I love coconut sugar and prefer to use it in most of my sweet recipes, I opt for an unrefined, lighter-color cane sugar for these custards. Coconut sugar is just a touch dark for this recipe.

Vanilla Bean Powder Note: I'm often asked why I use vanilla bean powder (see page 21). Here, it really is special. If, however, you don't have it, use 1 teaspoon pure vanilla extract.

Ramekin Note: My ramekins are 3 inches in diameter and almost 2 inches deep; I can fill 6 halfway or 5 about three-quarters full).

Serving Suggestion: Top with fresh berries or a dollop of Strawberry Sauce Forever, page 248.

Dreamy Fudge Sauce

This reminds me of the hot fudge sauce from Dairy Queen that we used to love as kids. I was the one who always ordered extra sauce. Since this version of a DQ-style sauce is dairy-free, I prefer to think that the D in DQ stands for "Dreena"!

Makes ¾–1 cup

¼ cup cocoa powder

2 tablespoons pumpkin seeds

1 tablespoon rolled oats

⅓–½ cup nondairy milk (see note)

¼ cup pure maple syrup

1 teaspoon pure vanilla extract

¼ teaspoon sea salt

Combine all the ingredients in a blender (preferably high-speed; see note). Blend on the soup function to puree and then warm and thicken the sauce. You may need to puree a little more depending on your blender. The sauce should be quite warm when finished. Transfer to a container to cool slightly, or allow to cool in the blender jar. The sauce will thicken more as it cools. Serve warm, or allow to cool completely.

Milk Note: This sauce thickens after pureeing. With ½ cup of milk, the sauce will be pourable, with just a slightly thick consistency. If you want a very thick sauce, use less milk, about ⅓ cup. Keep in mind that it thickens as it cools as well. You can also thin the sauce after it cools, stirring in a touch more milk. Almost any type of nondairy milk will work here, but with oat milk, the mixture can become too sticky and thick.

Blender Note: If you're using a standard blender, puree as long as needed to get a smooth texture. Once smooth, transfer to a small saucepan to warm and thicken over medium-low heat, whisking occasionally, until a slow bubble develops. Then, remove from the heat and serve hot or warm, or let cool and store in a covered jar in the fridge for up to 5–6 days.

Dessert Cashew Cream

Just as Cashew Cream (page 115) can be used to enhance many savory dishes, a sweetened cashew cream is just dreamy for desserts and breakfast dishes!

Makes about 1½ cups

1 cup soaked and drained raw cashews (see page 12)

Pinch sea salt

½ cup water, plus more as needed (see note)

2 tablespoons pure maple syrup, or more to taste

1½ teaspoons fresh lemon juice

½ teaspoon grated lemon zest (optional)

¼ teaspoon pure vanilla bean powder (optional)

Combine the cashews, salt, water, maple syrup, and lemon juice in a blender (or in a deep cup if using an immersion blender) and puree until very smooth, scraping down the blender as needed. If not fully smooth, puree again and add another few teaspoons of water if needed. Taste, and adjust with more sweetener as needed; stir in the lemon zest and vanilla bean powder if you like. Serve, or store in an airtight container in the refrigerator for up to 6 days. If you don't plan to use it within this time, transfer to the freezer.

Water Note: Usually ½ cup will be enough to yield a thick, velvety cream. However, if your cashews aren't as swelled, or if your blender isn't high speed, you may find it helpful to add another splash of water. Kept thick, it is perfect as a cream to dollop on pancakes and waffles. If you'd like to thin it, add more water a tablespoon at a time to reach the consistency you like. Thinned out, this cream is lovely drizzled over fresh fruit, Charming Apple Crisp (page 239), or Wow 'em Waffles (page 35).

Coconut-Date Caramel Cream

Everything into the blender, and presto—you have a date-sweetened caramel-like cream that's scrumptious on pancakes, waffles, and more!

Makes about 1½ cups

½ cup pitted dates (soaked if necessary; see note)

¼ teaspoon (generous) sea salt

¼ teaspoon pure vanilla bean powder

½ cup refrigerated canned coconut cream (see note)

½ cup plain or vanilla nondairy milk, divided, plus more as needed

Combine all the ingredients in a blender, using about half of the nondairy milk to start. Briefly blend to incorporate the ingredients, then add the remaining nondairy milk and blend again until smooth, adding a touch more milk if needed. Once smooth, blend a little longer to warm the cream. Serve right away, or let cool and store in an airtight container in the fridge for up to 5–6 days.

Date Note: If the dates are soft and pliable, there is no need to soak them—just put them in the blender as they are. If they are hard, soak them first in a bowl of hot water for 10–15 minutes to soften. Drain off the water, squeezing the dates a little to remove excess moisture, then add them to the blender.

Coconut Cream Note: Use regular (not light) coconut milk in this recipe. Before using, refrigerate the can overnight or for a few days. The thick cream will rise to the top and be easy to scoop and measure. Use only the thick cream (reserve the thin coconut milk for another use).

Serving Suggestions: Try this cream on Light and Fluffy Pancakes (page 59) or Wow 'em Waffles (page 35), or to top Guinnessless Sheet Cake (page 211).

Strawberry Sauce Forever

This sauce, or compote, is bright in flavor and color, and is easy to make. Enjoy it on desserts, or for breakfast dishes, or simply straight up with a spoon!

Makes about 2 cups

3 cups fresh or frozen sliced strawberries

1 cup fresh or frozen whole raspberries or more strawberries

½ cup chopped unsulfured dried apricots

Pinch sea salt

2 tablespoons freshly squeezed orange juice

½–1 teaspoon grated orange or lemon zest (optional)

Sweetener to taste (optional; see note)

In a saucepan, combine the berries, apricots, salt, and orange juice. Cook over medium-high heat until the fruit starts to break down and the mixture begins to bubble. Reduce the heat to medium-low, cover, and simmer until the fruit breaks down further, about 15 minutes. Remove from the heat and stir in zest (if using). Once the sauce has slightly cooled, taste, and if you'd like to add any sweetener, stir it in. Let the sauce cool fully. Serve immediately or transfer to an airtight container and refrigerate for up to 6 days.

Sweetener Note: The apricots add plenty of sweetness, and I like this sauce with a touch of bright tartness. However, depending on the sweetness of your berries, you may desire a touch of extra sweetener, such as pure maple syrup or coconut nectar. Wait until the sauce has cooled a little and taste it before you decide. If you want to add some, add just a teaspoon at a time.

Serving Suggestions: Serve this sauce on Mythical Cheesecake (page 236), Vanilla Custards (page 242), Wow 'em Waffles (page 35), or Light and Fluffy Pancakes (page 59). Also use it to make dessert or breakfast parfaits, layered with fresh fruits and Dessert Cashew Cream (page 246) or a nondairy yogurt.

2-Ingredient Watermelon Gelato

Watermelon gets even better when frozen and churned into this refreshing, sugar-free, dairy-free gelato. It's delightful!

Makes about 5 cups; serves 4–5

5 cups frozen cubed watermelon (see note)

1 cup sliced fresh or frozen overripe banana (see note)

½–1 tablespoon coconut nectar or other liquid sweetener (optional)

Put the watermelon and banana in a food processor or high-powered blender. Pulse to mince the frozen fruit into slivers or small pieces, then puree until smooth, scraping down the processor once or twice. Don't add any liquid to the puree! The watermelon is already so water-dense. Let the processor do its thing. Taste, and if you'd like it a little sweeter, add the sweetener as desired. Serve, or transfer to the freezer for an hour or more for a firmer set gelato (see serving tip).

Watermelon Note: Cube the watermelon and spread it out on a baking sheet lined with parchment paper to freeze. This will need to be done a day in advance (or longer) before making the gelato. Freezing the watermelon on the parchment rather than a container or bag keeps the watermelon chunks separate, making it easier to break up in the processor. After it's frozen, then you can transfer the cubed watermelon to a resealable plastic bag or airtight container until ready to make the recipe.

Banana Note: If you don't have a frozen banana, you can use fresh, since the bulk of the fruit (watermelon) is frozen in the recipe. When freezing bananas, don't freeze in the peel! It is very hard to peel after freezing. Just peel and slice up your overripe bananas, then pop them into a container or resealable plastic bag and freeze so they are always at the ready. Don't like bananas? Their flavor isn't pronounced here, and they do help make the gelato a little creamier. If you really want to omit it, you can; the finished texture will be a little grittier.

Serving Tip: This gelato is best enjoyed immediately, or after setting in the freezer for just an hour or so. If the gelato freezes longer, it will need to thaw slightly, and then the texture becomes a little watery.

Idea: Want some flavor variations? Replace 1–2 cups of the watermelon cubes with 1–2 cups of frozen raspberries or strawberries!

Maui Gelato

With purple sweet potato and a light hint of macadamia nuts, this chocolate treat brings back memories of Maui. It's rich and delicious!

Makes about 3 cups

1 cup cooked purple sweet potato flesh, cooled (see note)

¼ cup raw macadamia nuts

¼ cup rolled oats

¼ cup plus 2–3 tablespoons coconut sugar or date sugar

¼ cup cocoa powder

¼ teaspoon (scant) sea salt

½ cup vanilla or plain nondairy milk

⅓–½ cup refrigerated canned coconut cream (see note) or nondairy creamer

2 teaspoons pure vanilla extract

Combine all the ingredients in a blender (starting with ¼ cup or so of the coconut sugar) and puree until smooth. Taste and adjust the sweetness as you like (keep in mind that the mixture will taste a little less sweet when frozen). Transfer the mixture to a container to freeze for a few hours until set, stirring once or twice as it freezes. Alternatively, if you have an ice cream maker, you can churn it according to the manufacturer's instructions.

Sweet Potato Note: I bake these just as I do orange and yellow sweet potatoes (see page 11). Purple sweet potato is fun to use, but you can certainly use orange or yellow sweet potatoes. Yellow sweet potatoes are more similar to purple in texture. (Purple potatoes have the least moisture of these varieties; orange have the most.)

Coconut Cream Note: Use regular (not light) coconut milk in this recipe. Before using, refrigerate the can overnight or for a few days. The thick cream will rise to the top and be easy to scoop and measure. Use only the thick cream (reserve the thin coconut milk for another use).

Acknowledgments

To my readers: I've always said I have the best community. I do! Your notes of appreciation, support, and enthusiasm have meant so much to me through all these years.

To the BenBella team: It's been a delight to work with you all again. To Glenn Yeffeth, thank you for partnering on a second book and fostering such a warm and helpful team. I love working with you all! To Claire Schulz, thank you for your editing magic, and all of your insights and feedback. It helped me through my writing process as well as through all those super fun editing rounds! Thank you to Lindsay Marshall and Heather Butterfield for your continued support and expertise, from *Plant-Powered Families* through to this book. And, thank you (kindly) to all the other team members who helped bring this book to life: Katie Hollister, Jennifer Canzoneri, Leah Wilson, Sarah Avinger, Alicia Kania, Adrienne Lang, Monica Lowry, Rachel Phares, and everyone else at BenBella.

To John Robbins: It is so special to have you contribute a foreword for this book. *Diet For a New America* sparked my personal awareness, growth, and career. Moreover, your work embodies kindness, and you inspire so many to choose compassion in all areas of their lives.

To Dr. T. Colin Campbell: I consider you my nutrition godfather. It is a dream of mine to meet you in person, and I thank you sincerely for everything you have contributed, and continue to give, to our growing plant-based world.

To Ocean Robbins: I'm deeply grateful for your endorsement, also for your passion in sharing health and wellness with the Food Revolution Network. It was a privilege to work with you and all the kind people in your Whole Life Club.

To Brenda Davis: Thank you sincerely for your quote, and for writing *Becoming Vegan* way back when there were few resources for vegans. It was the book I turned to time and again when raising our daughters.

To Angela MacNeil: You were positive, willing, and enthused through the entire process. Thank you for the hard work you put in through a tight timeline, and for delivering such beautiful food photographs for us all to enjoy.

To Sarah Amaral: Thank you for a beautiful and joyful day of photography. You have an eye and a natural gift, and I'm grateful to be a recipient of that talent. Extended thanks to Steve and Trish Stew for preparing the most gorgeous and welcoming setting for our cover and interior photos.

To Daniela Fisher: Thank you for helping me remember and reconnect with my potential.

To my darling and devoted recipe testers: Molly Duffy, Amy Johnson, Nina Windhauser, Claire Engstrom, Dee Campbell, Cintia Bock, Monica Valencia, Laurie Bleeks, Cindy Read, Jenni Mischel, Michelle Bishop, Elaine Trautwein, Kimberly Roy, Monica McCue, Natalie Carpenter Collins, Christine Riggs Magiera, Michele Isaac, Eve Lynch, and Sarah Wise. This book would not be complete without you. I am deeply appreciative of all the time you devoted to testing these recipes, helping refine the recipes, and all your enthusiasm through the process. You are the chocolate to my tea! And, an additional thank you to Monica Valencia for offering the suggestion that became this book's title!

Finally, to my mother, my husband, Paul, and our daughters, Charlotte, Bridget, and Hope: Thank you for your support and love, always.

Recipe Picks

Wondering what the best recipes are for the holidays? How about potlucks? Which recipes freeze well? Here are my answers! These lists aren't exhaustive, rather they are some of my top picks. Also visit my site and other books for additional ideas. I have some longtime favorite recipes on my site.

POTLUCK PICKS

These recipes hold up well to prep in advance and tote to a potluck, and they keep well at room temperature (or can be easily reheated). Of course most of the desserts are good for potlucks, but I selected a few that would really stand out!

Salads:
Cornucopia Salad (page 62)

Rainbow Slaw (page 65)

Mediterranean Abundance Salad (page 74)

Picnic Pasta Salad (page 78)

"Couch Potato" Salad (page 80)

Fresh Fruit Salad (page 92)

Appetizers/Dips:
'Kin Queso (page 96)

What-amole (page 104)

Truffle-Salted Nut Cheese (page 106)

Soups/Stews:
Pressure Cooker Quicken Noodle Soup (page 120)

Curried Carrot and Lentil Soup (page 124)

A-Game Chili (page 130)

Casseroles/Stovetop:
Lofty Lasagna (page 161)

Lentil and Sweet Potato Meatloaf (page 179)

Chickpea Satay Casserole (page 180)

Sweet 'n' Sour Lentils (page 184)

Spanish Rice (page 188)

No Butter No Chicken (page 191)

Pressure Cooker New Year's Baked Beans (page 208)

Desserts:
Honest Chocolate Chip Cookies (page 214)

Nummy Brownie Bites (page 221)

Raspberry-Coconut Crumble Bars (page 222)

Dreena's Nanaimo Bars (page 226)

Yellow Sweet Potato Cake with Yellow Sweets Frosting (pages 229 and 230)

Mythical Cheesecake (page 236)

Charming Apple Crisp (page 239)

Heavenly Baklava (page 240)

HOLIDAY MENU

I created a number of holiday recipes for this book because it's a request I get so often; see the Holiday Fare chapter. This list includes some festive options from that section and other chapters. I think you'd be very happy to have these items for the holidays, and I've even included some ideas for food gifting!

Thanksgiving and Christmas

Gingerbread Granola (also lovely to gift!) (page 43)

Cornucopia Salad (page 62)

Holiday Dinner Torte (page 198)

Cran-Apple Compote (page 201)

Golden Gravy (page 202)

Lemon-Dijon Roasted Potatoes (page 205)

Roasted Squash and Sweet Potato Puree (page 206)

Guinnessless Sheet Cake with Coconut-Date Caramel Cream (page 211 and 247)

Heavenly Baklava (page 240)

Vanilla Custards with Strawberry Sauce Forever (page 242 and 248)

New Year's

Rainbow Slaw (page 65) or "Couch Potato" Salad (page 80)

Pressure Cooker New Year's Baked Beans (page 208)

Date-Sweetened Bundt Cake with Lemon-Maple Glaze (page 234)

RECIPES THAT FREEZE WELL

These certainly aren't the only recipes that freeze well in this book, but they are some of the top choices.

Silky-Smooth Applesauce (page 44)

Lemon-Poppyseed Muffins (page 48)

Sweet Potato Muffins (page 51)

Chocolate Chip Muffins (page 52)

Hope's Blueberry Muffins (page 55)

Chocolate Zucchini Bread (page 56)

Light and Fluffy Pancakes (page 59)

'Kin Queso (page 96)

Good Day Sunshine Hummus (page 99)

Truffle-Salted Nut Cheese (page 106)

Curried Carrot and Lentil Soup (page 124)

White Bean and Corn Chowder (page 129)

A-Game Chili (page 130)

Alphabet Soup (page 133)

Pantry Soup (page 134)

Beyond Beet Burgers (page 137)

Bistro Burgers (page 143)

Mamma Mia! Marinara (page 156)

Lofty Lasagna (page 161)

Pumpkin Seed Pesto (sauce only) (page 172)

Lentil and Sweet Potato Meatloaf (page 179)

Sweet 'n' Sour Lentils (page 184)

No Butter No Chicken (page 191)

Holiday Dinner Torte (page 198)

Roasted Squash and Sweet Potato Puree (page 206)

Pressure Cooker New Year's Baked Beans (page 208)

Shmoopy Cookies (page 218)

Nummy Brownie Bites (page 221)

Crackle Blender Brownies (page 225)

Dreena's Nanaimo Bars (page 226)

Yellow Sweet Potato Cake (page 229)

Yellow Sweets Frosting (page 230)

Mythical Cheesecake (page 236)

Dreamy Fudge Sauce (page 245)

Dessert Cashew Cream (page 246)

Strawberry Sauce Forever (page 248)

2-Ingredient Watermelon Gelato (page 251)

Maui Gelato (page 252)

Guide to Cooking Beans

Soaking beans before cooking them improves digestibility and hastens the actual cooking time. Beans can be soaked overnight (at least 8 hours but even longer is better, up to 24 hours), or they can be quick-soaked. For a long soaking, rinse the beans, put them in a large bowl, and cover with water. Change the soaking water at least once through this time. After soaking, drain the beans, rinse, and proceed with cooking.

Since cooking beans involves a little prep on your part, it's very useful to cook them in batches. You can refrigerate cooled beans in airtight containers for up to 5-6 days, or store in the freezer for several months.

For a quick soak, rinse the beans, put them in a large pot, and cover with water. Bring to a boil and let boil for 5–7 minutes. Turn off the heat, cover, and let sit for 1–2 hours. Drain, rinse, and proceed with cooking.

To cook beans, combine 4 parts water to 1 part beans in a large pot. Bring to a boil, then reduce the heat and simmer, partially covered, until tender (see the estimated times in the following chart; timing can vary depending on the size and age of the beans).

To aid in digestion, and to add subtle flavor to the beans, try adding a piece of fresh ginger or turmeric, a sprinkle of fennel seeds, and/or a strip of kombu seaweed during cooking.

Don't add salt while cooking; season after the beans are cooked through.

Once the beans are cooked and cooled, they can be portioned and refrigerated or frozen.

Bean and Legume Cooking Times

Legume	Cooking Time	Legume	Cooking Time
Adzuki beans	45–60 mins.	Lentils (red)*	15–25 mins.
Black beans	60–90 mins.	Mung beans*	40–50 mins.
Black-eyed peas	45–60 mins.	Navy beans	70–90 mins.
Cannellini (white kidney) beans	60–90 mins.	Peas, split	45-60 mins.
Chickpeas	1½–2 hours	Pinto beans	60–90 mins.
Kidney beans (red)	1½–2 hours	Soybeans	3–4 hours
Lentils (brown/green)*	30–40 mins.	*No presoaking needed	
Lentils (French/Le Puy)*	35–45 mins.		

In general, 1 cup dried beans yields 2½–3 cups cooked.

Guide to Cooking Grains

Rinse grains (excepting rolled oats) before cooking.

To cook, combine the grain and cooking water, bring to a boil, reduce the heat to low, cover, and simmer. About 5 minutes before the cooking time is complete, remove the cover and check for doneness. Once cooked, remove from the heat. Let stand, covered, for 4–5 minutes.

As with beans, it's useful to cook grains in larger amounts than you need for a specific meal. I generally cook beans in larger batches than grains. Beans freeze very well, whereas grains can become a little spongy/watery after freezing and thawing. So, I normally batch-cook enough grains for 2–3 meals for the week. Once the grains are cooled, transfer to airtight containers and refrigerate for up to 6 days.

Grain Cooking Times

Grain (per 1 cup)	Water Required to Cook	Cooking Time
Amaranth	2½–3 cups	20–25 mins.
Barley (pearl)	3 cups	40–50 mins.
Barley (pot)	3 cups	55–65 mins.
Buckwheat	2 cups	15–20 mins.
Bulgur	2 cups	5–10 mins.
Cornmeal (coarse, polenta)	4–5 cups	25–30 mins.
Cracked wheat	2 cups	20–30 mins.
Kamut	4 cups	70–90 mins.
Millet	2½–3 cups	18–25 mins.
Oat groats	3 cups	50–60 mins.
Oats (rolled)	2 cups	10–12 mins.
Oats (steel-cut)	3 cups	20–30 mins.
Quinoa	2 cups	12–15 mins.
Rice (brown basmati)	2 cups	35–45 mins.
Rice (long-grain brown)	2 cups	40–50 mins.
Rice (short-grain brown)	2 cups	40–50 mins.
Spelt berries	3 cups	55–70 mins.
Teff	3 cups	10–20 mins.
Wheat berries	3 cups	55–70 mins.
Wild rice	3 cups	45–60 mins.

In general, 1 cup of dry grain will yield 2½–3½ cups cooked.

Metric Conversion Chart

Volume Equivalents (Wet)

Standard	US Standard	Metric (Approximate)
2 tablespoons	1 fl. oz.	30 mL
¼ cup	2 fl. oz.	60 mL
½ cup	4 fl. oz.	120 mL
1 cup	8 fl. oz.	240 mL
1½ cups	12 fl. oz.	355 mL
2 cups or 1 pint	16 fl. oz.	475 mL
4 cups or 1 quart	32 fl. oz.	1 L
1 gallon	128 fl. oz.	4 L

Volume Equivalents (Dry)

Standard—Metric (Approximate)	
⅛ teaspoon	0.5 mL
¼ teaspoon	1 mL
½ teaspoon	2 mL
¾ teaspoon	4 mL
1 teaspoon	5 mL
1 tablespoon	15 mL
¼ cup	60 mL
⅓ cup	80 mL
½ cup	120 mL
⅔ cup	160 mL
¾ cup	180 mL
1 cup	240 mL
2 cups or 1 pint	475 mL
3 cups	700 mL
4 cups or 1 quart	1 L

Weight Equivalents

Standard—Metric (Approximate)	
½ ounce	15 g
1 ounce	30 g
2 ounces	60 g
4 ounces	115 g
8 ounces	225 g
12 ounces	340 g
16 ounces or 1 pound	455 g

Oven Temperatures

Fahrenheit (F)—Celcius (C)	
250°F	120°C
275°F	140°C
300°F	150°C
325°F	160°C
350°F	180°C
375°F	190°C
400°F	200°C
425°F	220°C
450°F	230°C

Subject Index

A
almond flour   20
almond meal   20
applesauce   20
aquafaba   24
arrowroot   18

B
baked goods   23–24
batch-cooking   5, 11–13
beans
    batch-cooking   12
    as cashew substitute   19
    cooking guide for   258
    makeovers for   14–15
breadcrumb makeovers   15
burger mixes, freezing   23

C
cashew substitutes   19
chickpea miso   18
The China Study (Campbell and Campbell)   3
chocolate   20–21, 23
chocolate chips   20
chopping fruits and vegetables   10
citrus zest   11
cocoa nibs   20
coconut cream   15, 19
coconut milk   15, 24
crouton makeovers   15

D
dark chocolate   21
dates   20
Diet for a New America (Robbins)   2

E
egg replacers   19

F
flax meal   23
flax seeds   23
flours   20
freezing foods   10–11, 23, 24, 257

G
garlic, sautéing   22
gluten-free recipes   20
grains
    batch-cooking   12
    cooking guide for   259
    makeovers for   14

G
hemp seeds   19, 23
herbs   18
holiday menu   257
hummus   23

I
ingredients   17–22
    makeovers for   13–15
    preparing   7–11
    sautéing   21–22
    substitutions for   17–21

K
kindness   1

M
maple syrup   20
metric conversion chart   260
milk, plant-based   18
muffin liners   22
mushrooms, sautéing   21

N
nut butter substitutes   20
nut cheeses   23
nutritional yeast   18
nuts
    soaking and roasting   12–13, 22
    storing   23
    substitutes for   19, 20

O
oil-free cooking   4, 21–22

P
pasta   13
plant foods   1, 3
potatoes
    batch-cooking   11, 12
    makeovers for   13–14
    substitutions for   18
potlucks, recipes for   256
preparing ingredients   7–11
produce
    sautéing   21–22
    storing   9–10
    washing   7–9

R
recipe renewals   5

S
sautéing   21–22
seeds
    as nut substitute   19
    roasting   13, 22
    soaking   12–13
    substitutes for   20
spelt flour   20
storing foods   9–10, 23–24
sugar substitutes   20
sweet potatoes
    batch-cooking   11–12
    makeovers for   13–14

T
tofu   17

V
vanilla bean powder   21
vegan diet   ix, 2–4
vinegar substitutes   19

W
washing produce   7–9
white wheat flour   20

Recipe Index

About the Author

Dreena Burton is an esteemed vegan cookbook author, with six solo cookbooks and two co-authored titles. She began her plant-kind life over twenty-five years ago, and has raised three daughters from birth on a plant-based diet. Dreena's trusted whole-foods recipes have been featured with groups including PCRM, Forks Over Knives, Blue Zones, The Food Network, and The Food Revolution Network. Dreena shares more of her recipes at dreenaburton.com.

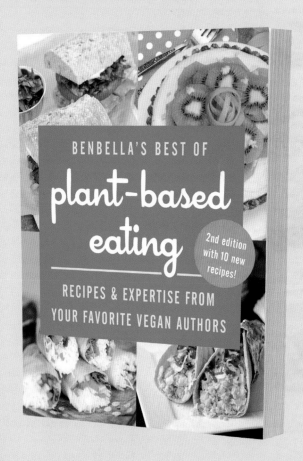

MORE DELICIOUS RECIPES FROM DREENA

FOR THE WHOLE FAMILY!

"*Plant-Powered Families* will revolutionize how you cook. Dreena's recipes are brilliant, combining nutrient-dense foods in imaginative ways to produce the most delicious, family-friendly dishes."

—GENE BAUR, president and cofounder of Farm Sanctuary and author of *Farm Sanctuary: Changing Hearts and Minds about Animals and Food*

"*Plant-Powered Families* is a great addition to any cookbook collection."

—T. COLIN CAMPBELL, coauthor of *The China Study*, *New York Times* bestselling *Whole*, and *The Future of Nutrition*

"Dreena's recipes are a triple threat: kid-approved, wholesome, and irresistible!"

—ANGELA LIDDON, author of the *New York Times* bestseller *The Oh She Glows Cookbook* and creator of OhSheGlows.com

"Dreena Burton's recipes and ingredients simply make good common sense. *Plant-Powered Families* is a great addition to any cookbook collection."
—T. COLIN CAMPBELL, PhD, coauthor of *The China Study* and the *New York Times* bestselling *Whole*

PLANT-POWERED FAMILIES

OVER 100 KID-TESTED, WHOLE-FOODS VEGAN RECIPES

Includes tips for pleasing picky eaters, whipping up DIY staples, packing school lunches & more!

DREENA BURTON
FOREWORD BY NEAL BARNARD, MD

AVAILABLE NOW WHERE BOOKS ARE SOLD.